1991-92

WANDA

Read By
Ella Fuchs
Gladys Sippert
Bette Durheim
Cheryl Brown
Bertha S
Friedrid
Herb. Miller

WANDA

by
Carol Anne Eby

Nazarene Publishing House
Kansas City, Missouri

Cover Design: Paul Franitza
Illustration: Keith Alexander

10   9   8   7   6   5   4   3   2   1

Contents

Foreword

YOU CAN'T REALLY capture the **whole** person in any book. Bits and pieces of their life can make a story. This is such a story—bits and pieces of an ordinary life with some "unordinary" happenings.

Carol Anne Eby has woven together the many hats worn by Wanda Knox in her interesting life—wife, mother, daughter, aunt, missionary, executive, and friend. Some hats will make you cry; others will provoke a smile.

Wanda loved life and squeezed into it and out of it every bit of excitement, challenge, and experience possible. She was so motivated by her deep love for the Master that she "forsook all, and followed him" (Luke 5:11). She believed that fun, fellowship, food, good books, beautiful scenery, and a continuous sharing of His Word were all His good blessings to be enjoyed to the fullest. And she did!

I first met Wanda when I became a member of the General NWMS Council. She was wearing the NWMS general director's hat, and her intense love for missions, missionaries, and the deep desire to provide education and motivation for young people to be **called** was obvious in her leadership role.

Wherever she went, with whomever she talked—over tea or tennis, Faith Promise or fellowship, study or Scrabble —the result was the same: a stimulated heart and mind. She challenged her hearers and her opponents to be and do their best.

—NINA G. GUNTER
General NWMS Director

1

Wanda Mae

THE RAYS of the late afternoon sun flickered across the
face of the little girl who resolutely clenched her fists to
brave once again the shadowy steps leading up to the attic.
In spite of being terrified of the spiders that lurked in the
shadowy corners, the prospect of the wonderful stories
awaiting her in the children's missionary meeting led her
on. Wanda Mae Fulton would never forget the junior Sunday School teacher who wept as she shared those missionary stories. She made the children actually hear the roar of
the lions, the cries of the lepers, and the pleading of child
brides. She made them feel the hopelessness of those who
didn't know Jesus. In later years as Wanda Knox, returned
missionary and executive director of NWMS, she would re-
count that story across the country. Her staff teased her

that as she shared with audiences, the steps got longer and the spiders more terrible; nevertheless, from very young childhood, she knew she wanted to tell others of Jesus.

Wanda was born March 21, 1931, in Oklahoma City. Her mother was 17 years old. A daily religious radio program that featured a Christian singer named Wanda inspired Mrs. Fulton for Wanda's name, and she added the Mae after Wanda's grandmother, who was to become a great influence in Wanda's life.

Wanda's family moved from Oklahoma City to Pauls Valley two months before her third birthday. There was no Nazarene church there at the time, so the family attended the First Baptist Church. When Wanda was six years old, Rev. M. L. Turbyfill came to Pauls Valley, purchased an old house, and started a Nazarene church. Wanda sang her first solo there, beginning a lifelong love for music.

Wanda's mother recalls that Wanda was saved and sanctified so early in life it almost seemed to her that Wanda was born a Christian, but Wanda recalled that important event very clearly. "In 1939 I gave my heart to Jesus—and somehow knew deep inside that *nothing* else in the world was worth living for. I was eight at the time, and this knowledge colored my thinking and my actions from that day on. Pauls Valley, Okla., and Rev. M. L. Turbyfill cared for *me*, a child. My heroes were not TV stars but godly men and women who consistently put Christ first—with *joy*. I guess it was their joy that spoke to me most."

Loving Jesus and the church did indeed consume Wanda's life from then on. She not only attended every meeting at the Nazarene church but also was a part of the Christian Endeavor, Baptist Union, and the Presbyterian youth groups during weekdays, and Youth for Christ on

Saturday nights. During the summer she would attend one Vacation Bible School after another. All the churches loved her. One afternoon the Presbyterian minister came by the Fulton household to tell Mrs. Fulton what a wonderful daughter she had. Wanda so loved and admired every evangelist and missionary who came to the church that she would cry and miss them for a long time after they left, which made her mother almost dread revivals.

When Wanda was 12, the family moved back to Oklahoma City. At this time Wanda became a charter member of the Shields Church of the Nazarene. Again, she became totally involved in the life of the church. She played the piano. She and her mom both sang in the services, solos because they both sang alto. There were "singings" at the different churches in those days, and Wanda never missed any. Every Sunday seemed to be open house at the Fultons. Dad Fulton would help with the cooking too, and the house was full every Sunday; if not an evangelist or missionary, it would be teenage friends. One was never enough. It had to be a group of at least half a dozen, and the more the merrier, even to 25 or 30, a pattern Wanda would follow the rest of her life.

Because Wanda and her mother were so close in age, often the mother-daughter roles seemed to be reversed. Wanda's mom recalls, "We would go to church camp at Turner Falls. I had a friend that had a little convertible, so we decided one morning we would go over to Ardmore to have breakfast. Wanda saw us leaving, so she stopped the car and said, 'Mother, where are you going?'

"I said, 'Over to Ardmore for breakfast.' I had to go through the third degree before I could go, for I had to be back for the service.

"After we left, my friend said, 'Who's the mother in this family?' When we attended church conventions together, we were both delegates, and of course I had to report to her where I went, even for a hot dog. But it was fun. I think they sent her along to protect me."

Wanda's ever-widening circle of friendships also included close ones developed in high school. Breathless, the girls often slipped into their desks at Capitol Hill Senior High just in time for class. Lunchtime had dissolved again into a long walk and a heart-to-heart talk with Wanda's best friend, Clyda. Other days, lunchtime would become serious study time as Wanda drilled Clyda on her biology (Clyda's least-favorite subject) to assure her passing the test. Wanda studied very hard and always made good grades. In addition to her devotion to studies, Wanda found time to be in the Girls Glee Club, Bible History Club, Spanish Club, and Debate Club. How she loved to debate! Clyda teased her that she could argue with a signboard. That honest questioning and earnest demand for answers would delight future college students as she challenged professors, perhaps frustrated or even exasperated mission directors and church superiors, but throughout her life she thirsted for truth.

When she was 16, Wanda's social life was blossoming, and finally Mom and Dad Fulton consented to let her go out. Later in the evening a slamming car door and running footsteps announced Wanda's return from her first date. The front door burst open. Wanda, looking very distraught, slammed it, backed up against it, and furiously proclaimed, "Mother, he tried to kiss me!" That overeager suitor was quickly dropped from the list.

Music filled Wanda's life. Loving to sing, she was a

member of the a cappella choir in high school and always involved in festivals and music contests. She played the alto sax and was first chair in Capitol Hill's band. She played at all the football games and then would spend the night at Clyda's house. While in high school, Wanda was asked to become the female member of the Forest Woodward Quartet. They sang on the radio each morning before school and traveled to many towns in Oklahoma on the weekend for concerts. Because Wanda was the only unmarried one, Clyda always went along as her guest. Any money left after expenses was divided. This was to be her spending money, but she always knew of someone who needed it more than she did or of some special project or offering that was coming up. Clyda declares that Wanda was the most unselfish person she had ever known.

In Wanda's reflections in her diary, she noted that her teenage years were good years. There were beautiful memories of a good home and good, solid parents; fun at school with friends to talk to and share deep things; understanding teachers; satisfying church services with growth in love of God's Word and of Him. She recalls men such as Rev. Louis McMahon, Rev. Willie Voight, Rev. Richard McBrien, and Rev. Joe Stevens, who, to an idealistic, searching teen, conveyed a sense of "total commitment" with joy. She remembers the beautiful little lady who always testified on Wednesday night with, " 'Bless the Lord, O my soul: and all that is within me, bless his holy name' " (Ps. 103:1), and the man who seemed to always end with, "It's a-gettin' gooder and gooder all the time!" Sometimes the teens laughed, but they couldn't miss the radiance on the faces or the kindly words of encouragement that Wanda always felt were for her.

Following Jesus and telling others of His love was a passion in Wanda's life. Yet during her teenage years she could not claim a mission call. Missionaries came and went, showed their slides, touched her heart. Missionaries such as Everette Howard and Louise Robinson Chapman stirred her soul, but a missionary call—no. Reminiscing, Wanda said, "My friends received one . . . nearly every missionary service sometimes. They would struggle, sometimes even lose out for a time, not wanting to go to the mission field. I remember praying, 'Father, I don't understand. Why don't You call me? I'll go—then they won't have to struggle!' But He never did."

In later years as Wanda watched teens struggle in a status-seeking, pressured age, she would say, "I didn't feel pressured as it seems so many youth do now—pressured to be the best at studies or at music or sports or at making money or making friends—winning teen talents and quizzes and popularity contests. No—I had time to reflect and to think and pray and take long walks and meditate and just be *myself*. No, I wasn't outstanding in anything. I just enjoyed it all—and in the process seemed to learn or discover that enjoyment of *Him* made *everything* sweeter."

In May of 1949, Wanda graduated from high school with honors, and in the fall was off to Bethany Nazarene College [now Southern Nazarene University], where she was to meet a young man named Sidney Knox and find a new name.

2

Mrs. Sidney Knox

THE COLLEGE DINING HALL hummed with the usual chatter of hungry students waiting for their lunch. Sidney Knox, a tall, serious-looking junior lost in his own thoughts, was suddenly brought back to the present by a bright, animated voice saying, "Mr. Knox, I really enjoyed your talk in missions class today." With a bright smile and a toss of the head, Wanda went on her way, but Sidney would never be the same. Heart pounding and lunch failing to digest very well, he raced to his room, sat down at the desk, and wrote Louise, his sister, these astounding words: "I met my future wife today. She doesn't know it, but she is." Thus began Sid's campaign to bring Wanda Mae Fulton to the altar to change her name, and he diligently pursued the cause with the same determination he used in every other task he faced. It wasn't long until Wanda accepted that first date, and soon they were spending a lot of time together.

They became part of an evangelistic team that went out on weekends, Sid preaching and Wanda helping with the singing. They early began to sing together and discovered they shared a lot of mutual interests. One such interest was a love for the children that they found in Shantytown and brought to Wanda's house to scrub down and clean up for Sunday School. Mom Fulton would help "scrub the tar" out of the children, pray that Wanda wouldn't catch lice, and smile at this tall, young man who was working his way into all of their hearts.

Sid and Wanda soon felt it was God's plan for them to become more than "good friends." Of course, Sid had felt God's leading from the first moment of their meeting, but Wanda needed a bit more convincing. Wanda, in love and radiantly happy, felt one burden: Sid had a call to the mission field. She didn't. Would this be a hindrance? Concerned, the young couple talked to Dr. Remiss Rehfeldt, the World Mission director at that time, and found that a wife could go on a husband's clear call—if she were willing. Wanda was willing!

May 27, 1951, was the most significant day of Sidney Knox's life to that moment, with the exception of the day he gave his heart to the Lord. That morning he received his college diploma, and that afternoon he met Wanda Mae at the altar to begin an adventure that would lead them to the "ends of the earth."

But for the next four years they went only as far as Texas. They began their ministry at a home mission church in Slaton and then after two years moved to Big Springs.

Geron Murray arrived on July 18, 1953, to bless the home.

While pastoring in Big Springs, the family attended the District World Missions Society Convention in Mineral Wells, Tex. Dr. Mary Scott was speaker and presented the challenge of New Guinea, a new field to be sponsored by NWMS. The offering for New Guinea was to be taken on October 15, NWMS day. Wanda reflects, "As Mary Scott spoke, my heart was stirred, challenged—and then heaviness set in. A heaviness that grew and grew—until before the evening, I knew I was being called to New Guinea. 'Why, Lord? Why now? I have loved You for years. I've been open to a call. Now I'm married. My husband feels a call to India. I must go with him. Why give me this heavy burden for New Guinea?'"

Wanda left the convention with a heavy, heavy heart.

The Knox family, 1955

During the next two weeks she prayed and wept much but couldn't shake the burden. She said nothing to Sid, but one morning he came into breakfast, looking a little "heavy" himself. Looking dejectedly at Wanda, he said, "I really hate to tell you this or ask you to go to such a primitive country, but I feel God is asking me to apply for New Guinea." Laughing, crying, and rejoicing, they fell into each other's arms; as Wanda said, "God always works on both ends (and in the middle, too, if He needs to)!" They applied for missionary work again. The board already had their application marked "Preference: India." Now it was "Preference: New Guinea."

They were asked to meet the Department of World Missions in January 1955. What excitement! The missionaries who had served a while shared experiences that encouraged the Knoxes; the new missionaries, like themselves, were apprehensive but knew they were obeying God to come this way. Meeting the board was eased by Sid's banter with Dr. Bob Mangum. When they met the general superintendents, Wanda remembered Dr. Samuel Young's astute question, "Do you plan to be one-term missionaries?" Wanda later said, "I'm so glad he asked that. It came in handy some years later!" Indeed, it was to be only a few years until this conversation was to be remembered and Wanda was to use it as a powerful, persuasive tool to continue her missionary career beyond one term.

The room was charged with emotional electricity. Hearts were beating madly under the young missionaries' calm exterior. The reading of the minutes finally came. At last their names were called. "Rev. and Mrs. Sidney Knox—New Guinea." As Wanda expressed it, "Oh my, oh my! Few times in life are so emotion packed. We knew the whole course of our life was now headed in a new direction. Congratulations, condolences; some of the older missionaries would really have enjoyed going with us."

The little family rushed back to Big Springs to begin preparations for leaving. October was the target date, and much had to be done. Overawed, perplexed sometimes, but never sorry, Sid and Wanda felt completely in God's will, and that was all that mattered. The Knoxes left Big Springs in May and attended the Summer Institute of Linguistics in Norman, Okla., from June until August. Deputation services followed, and they left Oklahoma City on September 26, 1955, Wanda experiencing her first plane ride. They flew to San Francisco, left there on October 5, spent a week in Hawaii with friends, then flew to Australia to spend three or four days in Sydney and two days in Brisbane. Finally, on October 14, they arrived in Port Moresby (MORZ-bee), administration headquarters of the Territory of New Guinea.

Wanda discovered early that missionaries' children are great ambassadors to win friends in other cultures. In later years, Wanda was to tell Geron how patient and good he was in those early days. After falling down the stairs in Hawaii and really frightening his parents, he won everyone's heart in Port Moresby. They all loved this little two-and-a-half-year-old American boy with his short pants, bow tie, and quick smile. The heat bothered Geron a great deal, and he woke up one morning singing "It Will Be Worth It All When We See Jesus." Sid and Wanda got a laugh out of that and spoke of it many times. "Out of the mouths of babes" (Matt. 21:16)—Wanda would remind the children many times how true those words were.

The utility truck pulled up in front of the Papuan Hotel, and out hopped Geoffrey Baskett. Tanned, slightly graying at the temples, congenial, and with a wonderful Aussie accent, he walked into the Knoxes' lives, and a friendship began that was to grow and flourish through the years. Geoff was house-sitting for Dr. Todd, an Australian physician working in Port Moresby who was away with his wife, Lucy, on holiday. When he heard that the Knoxes needed a home to stay in, he called around to offer his assistance.

Geron regressed from his good behavior just before they left the hotel; he saw a child with a small tin airplane just like his. He was sure the child had stolen his airplane, so he went across to claim his possession. Wanda had difficulty convincing him it was not his toy; his was in their room. She had to drag him upstairs, she laughing, Geron howling, to convince him. Geron came down later hugging his airplane, and peace was restored.

It wasn't worth their packing and repacking for such a short distance, so Geoff's first memories of Wanda were of her standing in the back of the utility truck, holding a number of dresses by their hangers, and laughing with Sidney as they drove through the streets of Port Moresby like people advertising a secondhand sale!

Remembering those days, Geoff recalls, "I have always enjoyed the fellowship God gave me with the Knoxes. Having them stay with me in Moresby was great fun as they made fun of my English expressions, and I pulled their legs about the things they did and said. Our different ways of attacking boiled eggs was often a topic of some concern on my part." Geoff expressed dismay at the barbaric American style of opening a soft-boiled egg. Americans attempt to crack open a soft-boiled egg as it rolls around on the plate rather than placing it into an eggcup where the end can be neatly removed. Wanda remembers that, too, and lists learning to eat boiled eggs properly as part of her Port Moresby memories. Others included: (1) ordering food from restaurant menus by numbers, (2) delicious papaya, (3) asparagus on toast for breakfast, (4) watery milk shakes, and (5) hamburgers with egg and beets. There was always "heat, heat, heat" but also a delightful ocean where they walked every day with Geron, who never tired of throwing rocks into the water. A CWA (Country Women's Association) guesthouse, where tea, biscuits (cookies), and sandwiches were served, and an Anglican church were places where they met many wonderful people, had good fellowship, and sensed warmth and love. While in Port Moresby, they helped Geoff celebrate his 40th birthday with chocolate cake. Wanda learned that was a "kid's" cake, and real birthday cake was fruitcake. They presented a Bible to Geoff with their names inscribed on it for his gift.

In December the Knoxes flew to Lae (LAY) and again took up hotel living. Their first Christmas in New Guinea was spent in the hotel. Geron substituted swimming in the pool for playing in the snow, and cold soda pop for hot chocolate, but a tiny artificial tree was presented as a gift from the hotel manager, and there were lots of cards and letters from home. Sid gave Wanda a Chinese cedar chest, and since the ship had arrived with their goods, Geron wanted to get his rocking horse off the ship immediately.

After days of praying, fasting, and investigating, Sid knew Kudjip (KOO-jip) was the place where God was leading, and the Knoxes moved closer to their permanent home by going to Goroka (guh-ROW-kah) in the Eastern Highlands. During those 10 days in Goroka, Wanda remembers "the coolness of the Highlands, morning and afternoon teas (maybe that's why I still have to watch my weight!), and always—satisfying, beautiful fellowship with my husband. How richly we were able to share spiritual things—he was an inspiration and teacher to me. And—he was fun."

From Lae the Knoxes' housing material was flown in several DC-3 loads directly to Minj. A grass house that had been a malarial control school became home in Minj; new daily routines were established, such as baked beans on toast for breakfast and cold showers in a little grass house with no door while Sid stood guard outside. From Minj to Kudjip (a place, in Wanda's words, "that was to grow and grow in my heart and mind and spirit until it truly became 'home'") was 12 miles of winding dirt roads against a backdrop of magnificent mountains. The prefab house was brought in plank by plank by carriers making a wage of 11¢ a day.

Sid built the bush church and the prefab house simultaneously. He used as much help (all untrained) as he could get but carried the bulk of the construction himself. Wanda remembered that it was fun to help nail floors, and she did all of the inside painting herself. Geoff Baskett arrived shortly after the erection of the new home and remembers that one of his jobs was to clean the paint off some of the windows with a razor blade.

The Knoxes and Geoff also spent time planting rows of strawberries, and many years later when Geoff relocated near Kudjip, he was to have plants from those beds to set out in his new garden. Years afterward, Geoff nostalgically commented, "I just wonder if there will be celestial strawberries to be planted anywhere; if so, I hope the three of us are given the honor of doing the planting together!"

The Kudjip station had become a bustling compound. The hospital was then a long shed roofed with grass thatch. Patients lay on mats, and three or four fires burned in the center of the building. Both Sid and Wanda spent a lot of time talking to the folk through an interpreter or in pidgin (trade language of most of the island). A school was started, and both Sid and Wanda taught. Dorms were built, and Wanda and Sid shared the new experience of being dorm "Mom and Pop." The boys (no girls at first)—undisciplined, fearful of spirits, unsure of these strangers in their midst, full of mischief but yearning for love—found a place in the Knoxes' hearts. As Wanda said, "We all learned a lot!"

Preaching posts were established: Kudjip in the morning and Kurumul (KUR-uh-mul) in the afternoon. Later Pokorump (PO-guh-rump) was squeezed into the schedule. On Geoff's visit, he went with them to the preaching posts. They took pity on him and gave him chocolate bars to eat while they fasted during the day's journeying to the services. The three spent a lot of time singing together. Sidney had a rich voice. Wanda sang alto, and Geoff tried his best with tenor. One of Wanda's fond memories came from a service at Kurumul while she and Sid were singing a duet accompanied by Sid's accordion. One of their fashion-clad parishioners, frustrated with the button-up-the-back style of her latest used clothing, stood up and raised her dress to the appropriate level for her baby to receive his lunch. Modestly clad in her New Guinea strings, she didn't seem to interrupt anyone's attention except the very amused special singers.

Sidney and Wanda often left the compound to go

walking into the bush, carrying a suitcase of medicine, steel axes for tribal leaders, and Bible stories to share with those they met. Wanda remembers, "I can never express the depth of feelings that came from time to time: . . . delight at the beauty, yearning for the people . . . fear of wild pigs and single log bridges, of the intense darkness that seemed many times to hold more than darkness. There was joy in first communication success, deep joy in women's classes of sharing, deeper joy in small indications of the Spirit's speaking and working."

There were good times, and there were difficult and frustrating times, like the time Sid lost the top joint of his finger. But he even joked about that, saying he had saved quite a bit of money as a result. When anyone in a church asked how much he was willing to contribute to a collection, he held up 10 fingers but only had to pay $9.95 due to the lost section!

In September of 1957, another wonderful event blessed the Knoxes' home; Jane Marie Knox arrived, truly Wanda's "gift from God," for only a few months later Sid became very ill. Janie completed the family of four. Many times Wanda would go home from school at recess time to feed the baby and find that Sidney had been there first. He would be carrying her around the station, talking to her as he did his work. He loved his blond, curly-haired, blue-eyed girl. Sid was always a family man. He had dreamed of having his own children, and now he had a special four-year-old boy and a new baby girl. What more could he desire?

Janie was four months old when Sidney became extremely ill. After tests on the coast and in Goroka, he had an operation, which revealed that his body was full of cancer. In God's timing, the Max Conders had arrived the morning after Sidney was struck with extreme pain, and in the months following they taught Sid's classes and carried on the medical and church work until the Knoxes' departure in June of 1958.

Sid's family met Wanda and Sid and the children in California, and the family took Geron and Janie to Lubbock, Tex., by car. Also meeting them in California was a large crowd of California Nazarenes, who sang "To God be the glory—great things He hath done." Sid was overwhelmed and exclaimed, "Praise the Lord for the privilege of being a missionary in the Church of the Nazarene!"

After Sid had tests in California, the family flew to Lubbock in a small chartered plane. The days that followed were very precious in some ways, very hard in others. Sid

Return welcome, June 1958

was in and out of the hospital, having another operation. They rented an apartment, and Wanda learned to give his shots. In September Sid sent Wanda downtown to buy a special teddy bear to celebrate Janie's first birthday. Bright eyes sparkled at his baby girl through the wan mask of illness, and Janie even at that young age seemed to know something was not quite right. She stayed by Sid a lot, and when the family would go for a car ride, she would stand in the front and reach back to hold his hand or his finger while he lay on the backseat. He loved it, and Wanda would tell him she wouldn't let anyone else hold his hand!

Prayers were bombarding heaven, and many thought that Sid would be healed. Wanda thought so too. In later years she said, "I look back only at this with regret, for I believe he knew. Several times he tried to talk to me about his 'going.' I'd hear none of it—felt that was not showing faith. Now, I wish we could have shared deeply his feelings instead of him protecting mine. How rich it could have been, for he was so ready to go if that's what God wanted."

The last day of Sidney's life was on a Sunday. All the family were there, and at some point in the morning he had them read the 15th chapter of John. Then he prayed. In the words of Wanda, "Such a prayer of trust and commitment—of rest in Him, even as his heart seemed to break for the people of New Guinea and for me and his children and his family—his voice grew stronger and stronger; I could not keep my eyes closed, for I just knew he was about to get up!" That day he ate better, he had only one shot, and he was fully alert. Shortly after midnight on Monday, October 14, exactly three years from the day they'd landed in New Guinea, Wanda was sitting beside the bed, holding his hand, when he began to talk what seemed to Wanda nonsense. Her heart fell. She looked at him but could not understand anything he was saying. She thought he was delirious, but as she looked at him, he read her face and said, "Don't you understand what I'm saying?"

"No, Sid, I don't."

He replied, "Well, doesn't it make sense to you?"

"No, Sid."

He looked at her for a moment and then said, "Well, it does to me." Then he said, "Release me." Thinking that was strange language but obeying, Wanda let go of his hands, and Sidney changed worlds.

Geron was 5, Janie 1, Wanda 27. Then began one of the deepest struggles Wanda's soul ever knew. Few knew what she was facing. Most thought she was taking Sid's passing extra hard, but it wasn't just his going. Wanda and Sid had discussed death before. They lived in potential danger all of the time. There was the possibility of a plane crash, an accident in the bush, or malaria, but the struggle came because God didn't answer the thousands of prayers that had come before Him. Did God hear? Could God hear? Did God care? Was there even a God? Could this young woman who had served God since the age of 8 now really believe? The struggle lasted several months, but even during the struggle Wanda felt a call or pull back to New Guinea. She met the board and they said wait. She did deputation work; she walked the floor at night; but there was no answer. Finally, she declared to God that she had to have some kind of answer. Maybe she would have to become an agnostic, for she couldn't pretend to believe something she didn't believe; and New Guinea must be out, for how could she go back and proclaim to others what she was not sure of herself. Again silence. But the next afternoon He spoke. "I could take you to the place—I wasn't even thinking about Him—when all of a sudden, He was there. Eye did not see, but my spirit saw. He didn't give me an answer of why He allowed Sid's death. People had been giving me all sorts of answers, but they didn't answer my heart's cry. But when He came, my spirit was subdued—I couldn't even ask any questions. But He said (and the spirit's ears heard), 'I'm here—I'm in control. Trust Me. Don't trust Me for what I do or for what I don't do; just *trust Me.*'" Writing those words in her diary 24 years later, Wanda explained that that trust had been enough for her in the hard times and the easy. God had truly been her Comfort, her Teacher, her Guide, her Helper, her Confidence, her Joy.

The years, since the time when God had opened to Wanda's eight-year-old insight that nothing is really worthwhile except following Him, had proven to her that everything had been made greater and sweeter and more fun. Wanda affirmed, "My work, my family, my friends, my hobbies—it all has gained pleasure and meaning through the priority of Him. I know what the scripture means: 'Seek ye first the kingdom of God, and his righteousness; and all these things shall be added unto you' (Matt. 6:33)." Wanda was soon to discover that God's will was to lead her to a challenging new assignment that in most people's eyes seemed impossible, but Wanda's trust was firm and secure.

3

Miss Wanda

THE PASSENGERS in the crowded cabin of the Qantas jet began waking up after a long night across the Pacific. The young woman in the front seat, however, looked wide-awake as she busily penned a letter, occasionally glancing at the sleeping cherubs beside her: chubby, active, seven-year-old Geron and three-year-old Janie with the Shirley Temple curls.

> Somewhere above the Pacific on a Qantas jet
> October 27, 1960
>
> I know this is a bit unusual, but I'd like to write myself a letter today—to read now and then during the next ... whatever time God allows us. The sun is just coming up, and as high as we are, it makes a beautiful sight. What beauties God has allowed us in this world

to enjoy. In a few minutes we'll be landing in Fiji—then on to Sydney. It hardly seems possible that we are again this close to our land of New Guinea. I've been letting my emotions have full sway for the past few days and hours. I had really dreaded San Francisco; but instead of the depression I had expected to feel, I felt more of a release, as if a new inner assurance came that I was doing the right thing. . . . As we walked down the same ramp that Sid and I had walked up two years ago—again, instead of the feeling of pain I expected, I felt only joy. Along the way . . . I'm remembering our laughter together, our thrill, our fears, as we came out for the first time. Sid really seems quite close to me. I'm praying that God will keep this feeling of fulfillment within me, and that He will help me lean more and more upon Him that I might be able to fulfill the purpose He has for us in New Guinea. "Not by might, nor by power, but by my spirit, saith the Lord." Our cry? Give us souls. . . . Now unto Him that is able to do exceeding abundantly more than we can either think or ask; to Him we commit our whole beings and unto Him be honor and glory and praise forevermore. Amen.

WANDA KNOX
GERON AND JANIE

Wanda sighed, laid down the pen, and closed her eyes for a few moments of quiet contemplation. She thought back to that Saturday in January when she met the board to make her plea to return to New Guinea. The meeting had been difficult. The board members were very concerned about her welfare as a single parent with two small children and began to point out the problems and difficulties that would confront her. They felt that for her own good she would be better off in America. When the board members had finished their efforts to talk her out of going back under such trying circumstances, Wanda replied, "Sirs, I do not know what you are talking about when you speak of all the problems and difficulties and trials. I only know that God has called me to go back to New Guinea." The meeting ended, but Wanda was kept in suspense until Monday afternoon when the appointment was read in the general meeting that she was to return to New Guinea. In a letter to Wallace and Mona White, Wanda rejoiced: "Oh me, I can't even describe my feelings. It had seemed once as if the decision would go the other way. I realized there were problems involved and much indecision on the part of some, but Mrs. Chapman told me of how God opened the way for her to speak of some things that had been on her heart for some time, and then how He came in an unusual way. So I feel more than ever that it is of God! And, of course, that means much to me."

The board also voted that Wanda's return be delayed until fall so that a house could be put up for the family. That decision was harder for her to accept, for she was so eager to return that she would have been delighted to live in a bush house. However, Dr. Powers, having seen the New Guinea bush houses, felt very uneasy about such a situation. Wanda was made a delegate to the General Assembly to be held in June, so that helped stem her impatience a bit. It was her first opportunity to attend a general convention, and she was excited.

The Assembly was a great blessing to Wanda, reflected in her greetings to Mona White from Kansas City: "How easy it has been to sing from the bottom of the heart 'How Great Thou Art' as we've worshiped with some 17,000 Nazarenes from around the world. My heart has been stirred, my vision enlarged, and my faith increased. I've been praying that the surges of blessing that have swept over the crowd from night to night may not stop as we leave here, but may they spur us to take the fire with us to our various places to drop all superficiality and see the urgency of our day."

From June to November were trying days for Wanda. A merry-go-round of miscommunication seemed to be taking place. Wanda was waiting for a date of departure from the department, the department was waiting until the field notified them that Will Bromley had started the work in the Jimi, the field was waiting for the department to clear plans for the Jimi Valley project before Will was sent, and everyone seemed to be talking in circles. Kansas City was having a change of personnel; there was confusion over the housing situation on the field; and as Wanda said, "Everyone was confused (except me). . . . Well, I was in a convention in Georgia with Dr. Powers September 6, and we got it all straight, I think. I now have my passport and have just finished the last visa papers, so it should only be a few days until we board the plane for 'home.'"

And now home they were, and this arrival was quite different. The mission staff had now increased to five missionaries: Max and Mary Alice Conder, Wallace and Mona White, and Will Bromley. Five preaching points had been opened. A dispensary had been built, supervised by Mary Alice Conder, and during the previous year she had treated more than 2,000 patients with two New Guinean helpers as her only assistants. The Knoxes were welcomed warmly by

Wanda, Geron, and Janie boarding Qantas Airlines plane for New Guinea, October 25, 1960

both the missionaries and nationals. The people loved Wanda so. Wherever she would go, they would greet her with shouts and hugs as she stepped out of the jeep. For a while after her return, she had many tender and tearful meetings with those she had come to serve. They wanted to hear about Sid: his sickness, his death, his burial, his going to heaven. She talked to them mostly of his being in heaven now with Jesus and how he would someday meet her and them there because they would believe and become Christians too. It was glorious to see.

In New Guinea the school year begins in February, so Geron and Bob and Steve White started to school at Banz public school for Australians. Either Wanda or Wallace and Mona drove them back and forth each day. Little Janie would ride along. A few months after the Knoxes' return on one of the morning school runs, Janie looked up at Mona and said, "My daddy's in heaven, Aunt Mona; did you know that?"

When Mona reported her words, Wanda with great feeling replied, "What a blessing when she says that! God has given me so much. Mercy! What a good life I have, and I'm so happy He has let me come back here."

Mona (thinking back to the tragic loss of Sid) replied, "But I wonder how you can say it—"

Wanda interrupted, "Because of Sid's death? But don't you see? God goes ahead with His plan for my life. At first I took it so hard I almost didn't make it for about six months. Then I began to see how God was using it to touch many young hearts to give their all, as Sid did. And He continues to call me now to serve Him here. How good He is to me!"

Wanda began teaching in the mission primary school in February, and Janie played around her classroom door or went off with Uncle Wallace as he worked on the generator or went out in the jeep. Wanda was a good teacher. Nancy Seale, a primary teacher in later years, remembers that Wanda had only to arrive at the door, and the whole class was attentive, waiting to see what she would do. Nancy woefully added, "Mine—I could jump and yell, and they hadn't noticed I arrived!"

It was an intriguing adventure to introduce eager young minds to a wealth of knowledge outside the boundaries of their primitive world. Wanda was completely surrounded by excited little boys the first time she brought her typewriter to the classroom in hopes of catching up on her correspondence during recess. They were fascinated as they watched words go onto the paper. It seemed like magic!

Wanda was a motivator; she made learning a joy. She was an excellent teacher and really had fun at it, enjoying her students. She wanted to put herself into her work and could not enjoy a too-crowded schedule that wouldn't allow her to do her work well. Mona White noted, "She motivated an eagerness to learn not only in the classroom but also in everyday life. Among associates her happy enthusiasm and obvious enjoyment could spark a new interest in something or other (a subject, a theme, a method) till we were all curious and anxious to give it a try."

In the early 1960s, the New Guinean government was eager for the missions to establish up-to-date, outstanding educational institutions and granted subsidy to the missions to do so. Wanda wanted the Nazarene schools to rank with the best and took some rather drastic measures to achieve that excellence. Missionaries were allowed to teach without a college degree, but a crash course called the E course was being given at Rabaul at that time to upgrade the quality of teaching. The official name of the course was the Australian Condensed Teachers Course and was the equivalent of two years of teachers' training in two months. Wanda decided to go. It meant leaving Janie for several months, which was a great sacrifice for her, but in the loving care of the Whites, Janie was able to "loan" Mommy for a little while. Geron accompanied Wanda, as he could attend school, and a special treat for him there was being taught to swim by Geoff Baskett, who was visiting the islands with a group from the United church. Later Mona White also attended the course, and Wanda became resident mom to the missionary kids. To get her Australian Teacher's Certificate, Wanda took a series of 15 exams, 3 exams daily, two hours each, which showed her pursuit of excellence.

Teaching wasn't always easy. Wanda shared with her dear friend, Ginny Griffin, "You know, I'm enjoying school a lot more now. It took me a while to get adjusted back to grade school again. I love the kids and enjoy them no end in Sunday School or Vacation Bible School, but in school— I just don't seem to have the patience. If they want to learn, I have no trouble; but when I have to force them to, I just lose interest. And of course these kids have no parents behind them. The parents couldn't care less whether or not they learn." That attitude would change in later years, of course, as parents learned the economic advantage of a good education. In a later letter she would exclaim, "Sometimes I despair (everything they learn is in a foreign language . . . and also foreign to their culture), but then at other times they make me really proud. I'll really be proud if they just will all become Christians. We have a school revival coming up the last of this month. Remember to pray for the kids."

One of those answers to prayer was Merilyn Bukas, who lived on the station as a child. Very bright and eager to learn, Merilyn sold kaukau (COW-cow)—sweet potatoes —to earn her school fees. Miss Wanda was very special to

Merilyn. She taught her of Jesus, which transformed her life; she taught her harmony and helped train a lovely voice coming out of a background of monotonous chants; she modeled joy that was reflected in Merilyn's voice and face as she sang. Merilyn was to go from primary school to Mount Hagen (HA-gun) to complete grade eight and then to Madang, where she topped her class in secretarial training. In the intervening years she has worked at the district office and held sound jobs in Port Moresby, where she now resides and where she is an active laywoman in the Port Moresby church.

As years passed, Wanda's involvement with the schoolchildren extended beyond the classroom. Excerpts from letters tell of her full schedule. "I'm really busy just now. After this two weeks, things should slow down a bit. End-of-school picnics, Christmas plays, cantatas, parties, etc.—very time-consuming. To say nothing of dozens of tests to be marked! Oh well, the life of a teacher!"

Choir performances and dramas directed by Wanda were eagerly anticipated by both participants and audiences. Speaking of one such event, she wrote, "Our play turned out really well this year. We ended up giving it three times. Our first scene was Adam and Eve being tempted by Satan and falling. You should have seen it—the two who were Adam and Eve were all dressed up in leaves, and the crowd nearly came down with the snake—they all really acted well. Anyway, it ended (that scene) with God's putting them out of the garden but giving the promise—that though the snake had bitten their heel—'Another' would come to bruise the head of the snake. Then scene two started with Mary and Joseph and showed Christ to be the fulfillment of that promise. I really enjoyed working on it, and the students did too."

Another big interest of the children was sports, and in 1964 at last Kudjip triumphed. "We just got back from Minj, and I look like a beetroot. This was sports day, and Nazarene Mission really got on the map this time. We took the Trailblazers in their uniforms, and Ray [Bolerjack] marched them down the road with all the other kids following behind, and Gesip (GET-sip) marched in front with a big Nazarene Mission flag that Lee [Eby] made for us. The events were really well organized for the first time [thanks to the new Papuan supervisor], and the kids had a wonderful day. There were places all marked off for each school, and enthusiasm ran high. They provided lunch for everybody in an orderly fashion right up in front of the European Club. Anyway, eight schools entered. Minj came first, of course, with 120 points; Banz Lutheran came second with 95 points, and we came third with 92 points. We were second all the way until the last relay, so the kids were a little disappointed; but I tried to tell them how overjoyed they should be to have done that well! It was fun—but I wouldn't want to do it every month!"

Wanda's teaching abilities were also demonstrated in teaching both literacy and literacy teachers. She was a fluent pidgin speaker and went to work on the vernacular right away. She was good at it. She had taken a language course with SIL (Summer Institute of Linguistics) and was equipped to work on the language, but her constant frustration was the busy schedule that restricted her study. In a letter to the Wallace Whites, who were on furlough in 1964, she wrote, "I'm hoping I might get to spend some time in the bush this holiday. I said earlier in the letter that

I hadn't been frustrated lately; I'd better qualify that. I stay frustrated over the language. I have been trying so hard, but I'm just not enough [able] to do it without more help and more time to speak it. I've been doing all my services in place talk until it's time to give the story or message, but that's such a limited scope. I do get pretty discouraged over that sometimes. But I try not to let it defeat me."

Wanda never professed to be a preacher, but her teaching of God's Word displayed a deep love and faith. As she stood before a group of schoolchildren in chapel services, a class of new Christians in a membership class, or a congregation of worshipers, one could see in their eyes and from their faces that they were hearing, that they were "getting the message," catching some of the heartthrob of her own feelings, her love for God.

In one of her letters home, Wanda rejoiced, "We are so thrilled at how His Word is speaking to our folk. Keep praying for all our Christians especially—that the joy and strength they are finding will abound more and more, and make people hungry for what they have." And in another letter concerning camp meeting, "We have been having a good spirit here too—and are especially looking forward to our camp meeting next week. My, I wish you could be here for it too. The people have built beautiful grass 'long houses' to sleep in, with a courtyard in the middle for cooking over the open fire; our tent has arrived for services, and we have two really good speakers slated—I can hardly wait! I do hope we get in a lot of unsaved, as well as our Christians moving 'up.'"

Wanda realized that for the church to grow and mature, it would be necessary to have indigenous leadership. She felt this so keenly that those closest to her were influenced by her concern. When the Bible school first opened in 1964, one of those first students was Philip Kwonga (KWONG-uh), whom Wanda had urged to enroll, though it meant losing him as her kitchen help. Philip has faithfully served as a pastor for over 20 years. In the future, she was to lose two more cookboys to the Bible school: Mek and Joel.

Upon completion of the Nazarene Hospital, Kudjip, Wanda found a fulfilling ministry in hospital visitation. She visited the hospital often and made many friends. She endeared herself to the patients by bringing them food or some small gift, and "Miss Wanda" was loved by all. As she passed through the wards, she would stop at each bed to pray for the patient and his family. Often she would pick up a baby and carry it in her arms as she visited in the wards. Carolyn (Parson) Hannay, one of the missionary nurses serving in the hospital, remembers that it was always a fun time when Wanda came to visit. Carolyn remembers, "Even before we saw her, we would hear laughter and see a crowd gathering around someone, then see Wanda or hear her infectious laugh. They all called to her, for each one wanted her to come sit on his bed and listen to his stories of his family or village. She would listen, laugh, pray, and quietly move on to others. Actually she ministered to all in the ward as she tried to minister to each one, for all eyes were on her as she moved through the open wards."

Though Wanda had enjoyed all of her teaching assignments, the ultimate satisfaction and overwhelming joy was experienced in her assignment to the Bible college. Nudged by the Lord, while on furlough in the early 1970s, she wrote Wallace White. "I do hope you are considering seriously my last letter. I have been praying about the situation —and somehow I just can't feel clear about the English school. . . . I'm scared to death that I'll get put in and never taken out! I'm afraid I can't do it this term, Wallace. You know how I felt when I left—but when I felt definitely led to return, it seemed all tied up in a new burden for the Bible school and the feeling that I believe I have something to give there this term. Is that bad? I'm not trying to be difficult. I'm just laying bare my heart. Please do what you can." Meetings were held, schedules looked at, road conditions considered, available housing noted, and word returned to Wanda that if she could teach again in the English school for half a year, then she would be transferred to the Bible college. A worried Wanda replied, "I'm very disappointed about having to teach in the English school again. I really felt when I left I had to have a change this time. I've taught there ever since it began, and I think I have a bit of a hang-up on it."

Letters crossed in the mail, and Wallace teasingly replied, "Doc, you don't even wait to get my reply to your letter regarding your assignment—and you've written again. I think you are trying to underline and emphasize! No, seriously, I think you will have received the reply by now, and I have talked to Lee since that last letter, and we certainly are going to give it serious consideration." Finally, the Lord and Wanda prevailed, and Wanda was to triumphantly and joyfully announce to her friend Ginny, "I'm headed back to N.G.; I think I told you about the letter saying I'd be going straight to the Bible school—great!"

As Wanda began teaching, her joy increased more and more. In her letters home, she would tell again and again of her contentment with her assignment and the joy of be-

Wanda teaching in the Bible school

ing a part of the Bible students' lives. "Never have I had such joy and peace and contentment. The Lord has given me a double portion of it, and how I praise Him. Every day at the Bible school is a delight. Riding the Honda the nine miles up each morning and down each afternoon has also been a delight. The fellowship with the missionaries (all of them), our prayer services, the fellowship with our national people—somehow everything has taken on new meaning and new freshness. How grateful I am for this extra benefit from my Father. He has given more burden—more ache— and yet more depth of joy. See, you can't explain these things on paper! Can you read my heart?"

Opening God's Word to the Bible school students was a challenge and joyous opportunity for Wanda. One day as they were reading orally from a portion of Scripture, an audible groan broke out in the class. It moved Wanda to say, "Man, when God speaks to hearts through His Word that way, it really does something to me." Another day the class was discussing some points in Luke. Wanda, retelling the incident, said, "The guys were asking all kinds of questions (was I ever thankful for commentaries I'd read!), and we'd gone 20 minutes overtime. Finally, I said, 'We've got to quit—it's well overtime for next class.' One very promising fellow (I think will make a leading pastor) said, 'Well, if I am really hungry, and I see some good food there on the fire—I just want to finish it!' I could have hugged him."

Wanda's busy schedule, which covered 3 hours of New Testament survey, 3 hours of topical studies, 4 hours of music, and 2 of Scripture memorization, also included 15 hours of instruction for the wives. Such topics as Bible study, music, gossip, etc., were covered. Curtains, tablecloths, and pictures were made for the houses, and the wives were encouraged to keep their homes clean and freshen them up with flowers!

There were disappointments as well as victories. In one of Ginny's letters Wanda reported, "We've had a rough term in Bible school this last half of the year. The old enemy is sure fighting. But we've had some real breakthroughs, so we aren't discouraged. The more I teach here, the more I love it, but I know I get a lot more out of it than the students do. God has just poured out blessings on me. In spite of difficulties in several realms (can't put it all on paper—need to talk), loneliness for Geron and Janie (away at school; my house seems awfully big and empty), and a heavy work schedule—I have never known the way to be any sweeter. Isn't He good!"

One way Satan discouraged Bible school students was the clan influence upon their lives. Individuality is not encouraged. The clan is the important thing, and everyone is supposed to do and say those things that will help the clan as a whole. Others make it really rough on anyone who deviates from this rule. Wanda recorded an incident in one of her student's lives that showed how the Lord enabled him to stand apart for Christ. Gandi had gone home for vacation time, and to celebrate the occasion, all the men were sitting up "storying." All of a sudden, a little after midnight, a rooster crowed close to the house. All of the men (except Gandi) rushed excitedly from the house, knowing that the only reason a rooster would crow at that time of night was because a spirit was haunting the house. The men captured the rooster and made preparations to kill it to appease the spirit representing the dead ancestor. Failing to do this, they believed, would bring death to one of them. Gandi tried to witness and talk them out of it but to no avail. The rooster was caught, killed, and cooked. They believed the spirit would eat the spirit of the rooster and leave the meat for an unexpected feast for them. They asked Gandi to pray over the meal, but he refused. They argued with him that if he didn't participate too, then someone might still die, but he still refused. Soon after this, Gandi's mother became very ill. They brought her to the hospital, and the tribe put a lot of pressure upon Gandi, for they felt he was responsible. However, Gandi kept faith and prayed much. The missionaries prayed too, for they knew how Satan used such situations to break down young, newly budding faith. The tribe wanted to bring a poison man to work magic upon the ill woman, but again Gandi refused, saying, "No, we'll just keep praying. God can help her." God honored Gandi's simple faith, and his mother did get well and returned to her village. Gandi returned rejoicing to Bible school. That was not the last test Gandi had to face, but his faith remained strong, and today he fills an important position of leadership as district superintendent of the Chimbu (CHIM-boo) District and was one of the Papua New Guinea delegates at the 1989 General Assembly.

Life was certainly never dull on the mission field. Screams and shouts rent the air, disturbing the serenity of the mission station on one quiet, peaceful afternoon. Wanda, turning into her drive from a service with high school students in Mount Hagen, noticed a lot of commotion up near the airstrip and started to go and investigate. Marjorie Merritts and Shirley Howes, missionary teacher and nurse respectively, running down the road, stopped her with a shout, saying, "We've been sent to your house [center of the station] for protection!" The Wabag tribe from the Southern Highlands and the local Kuma (KOO-ma) tribe had had a confrontation, and a real war had flared with arrows and spears flying thick and fast. They fought for about three hours; however, only six or seven casualties were brought into the hospital. These warriors were badly cut up and bruised (they also throw big stones), but at that time no one had died. Wanda had an amazing reaction. "Actually, I haven't watched a fight so closely before; it was fascinating. It was so much more humane than our 'civilized' warfare. Each tribe was yelling furiously and insulting the other . . . but one would gather on top of a hill, and the others in the tea fields below. They'd shoot arrows and spears until one tribe felt they were getting hit pretty hard and they'd retreat, and the other would chase them. Then they'd reassemble somewhere else and do it again. Everyone was totally involved; there was no cold calculation of wiping out the whole tribe from afar. Then, when it became dark, they'd call it off for the night, and so far today it hasn't flared again. Now, don't get me wrong; I'm not advocating wars and fights here! It's just that it reminded me of what I think Old Testament wars must have been like. It was like stepping back into a Philistine-Israelite time."

The years 1960 to 1975 were replete with rich, fulfilling ministry for Wanda. From the altar of that small home mission church, to a Christian college, to a parsonage, to the rugged terrain of Papua New Guinea, she had followed the leading of her heavenly Guide. Along the way she had experienced disappointment, heartache, sorrow, and pain, but also she had experienced deep satisfaction, peace, and always deep joy. In a letter home shortly after her return from furlough in 1972, she reflected those emotions. "How could I possibly describe the feeling I have within right now? I am sitting in my office, looking out toward the mountains, watching the people pass on the road. . . . I've just completed my lesson in New Testament survey to give at the Bible school tomorrow, and my heart is overflowing. I have never before had such a burden for our people even in the beginning, dark days. It seems there is a continual 'ache' deep down inside me somewhere that constantly breathes a prayer, 'O God, open their eyes, show them the truth of Thy Word; make them wise watchmen, tender shepherds, joyous Christians.' And yet along with this burden and ache, there is a contentment and peace deeper than I have ever known before. . . . The wells of joy are truly running deep, almost to my bewilderment at times. Somehow I have a strange feeling that this is a beginning of expectancy, the current in the air that the time is so ripe for our King's return." God was soon to change the direction of Wanda's life and ministry, but as always, where He led she would follow.

4

Mrs. NWMS

THE ROOM HUMMED with happy, animated conversation. The table was filled with mouth-watering goodies, and MKs in all sizes sat cross-legged on the floor, chattering and playing games. Meanwhile, their parents were catching up on all the stateside news that the returning missionaries were sharing. Lee and Carol Anne Eby and their four children were being welcomed home from furlough. Wanda, usually the leader of such discussions, sat at the edge in a rather pensive mood. In the midst of a crowded room, she and the Lord were in a discussion.

Since March she had had a period of uncertainty descend upon her. Wanda's very intimate relationship with God made her often say she thought she was a mystic in that she sensed a very special awareness of the presence of

God and His leading. Once she had even used mysticism as a bridge to witness to a Muslim. So in these ensuing months, she had asked the Lord, if she were not to return to New Guinea, to please let her know ahead of time if possible. Then she could tie up loose ends and leave the field, knowing she had completed her work. On this warm August evening, He let her know. Wanda explained, "At the Ebys' welcome home evening, I knew, just like that, that I wouldn't be returning. It was just as clear last time that I was to return, and what a glorious term this has been."

Like Abraham, Wanda began to prepare to go out, though she did not know her destination. She only knew that when the Lord said, "Go," she was to follow. She shared her feelings in a letter home to Ginny Griffin. "I have been taking things in to the full since August 1. . . . It has been sweet. Only a few people here knew. Even Wallace didn't know, for I knew Dr. Johnson and Dr. Lewis were coming in February, and I felt I should tell Dr. Johnson first—and I didn't want to write it; I wanted to discuss a lot of things. No one at home (except Geron) knew, and I told him not to mention it at all. I had planned to ask Dr. Johnson if there was some work in the missions office I could do, bookkeeping or some such. If there wasn't, I planned to try Olivet [Nazarene University], since Janie will be going there. When I arrived back from our Madang trip, I found this telegram waiting for me, saying I had been elected to be executive director of NWMS, as Dr. Mary Scott was retiring, and to call immediately. I was floored . . . and at first was going to refuse, for I still feel inadequate for such as this. But as I was praying that evening before calling the next day, I felt as if the Lord was saying, 'You were going to ask Dr. Johnson for a job; I have given you this one.' So what could I do? I still feel scared to death, but I am utterly amazed at God's timing. I've been a missionary for 20 years and have lost contact with a lot of the stateside activities; but if He has given me the job; then He will provide the strength and wisdom that I need to do it—in His way."

When Dr. Johnson arrived, Wanda did accept the position. Mary was to retire officially March 1, 1975, but was willing to stay on until Wanda could come and get settled. The only "fly in the ointment," as Wanda expressed it, was that Janie, because she was graduating from high school, would be unable to leave until after June 20. Finally, plans were arranged. Wanda would leave Kudjip in mid-March, spend a few days with Janie at Ukarumpa (OOK-a-rum-pa) where she attended high school, spend a few days in Australia and Canada, and then go straight to Kansas City, where Geron (in college at MidAmerica) would meet her. May 1 was the date set for her to be in the office. Dr. Lewis encouraged Wanda to do her visiting and vacationing before she got to Kansas City, for after she got into the office, it would be "quite a spell" before she could leave again. Wanda responded by declaring, "Man, I have so much to learn. I sure am glad I am certain this is in God's plan, or I'd be even worse scared!"

Janie would remain in New Guinea to graduate and then travel home with a family and three of her school buddies. A promised visit to Disneyland helped ease her disappointment at Wanda's missing the graduation, and plans were made to be reunited in June.

Wanda found that pulling up stakes after 20 years was a bit more difficult than she had anticipated. People that she had known for so many years kept coming by to say good-bye and give her chickens and presents to express their love and sorrow at her leaving. Wanda acknowledged their love by saying, "They're sweet, but it makes me feel . . . oh, you know. When you've stayed this many years in a place, it really does become a part of you."

Wanda was so caught up in packing and preparations for leaving that she was unaware of the many behind-the-scenes plans being made for her farewell. On March 7, 1975, Carol Anne Eby was to write, "Twenty years' service is over, but an exciting new experience lies ahead for Wanda. We did it! We did it! Seventy people were involved, but we completely surprised her. What a lovely evening."

Wanda walked into a classroom that had been transformed into a New Guinean paradise where missionaries and their families, friends and acquaintances from other missions, and friends from the Wahgi (WAH-gee) Valley community were sitting on mats at "banana leaf" tables trimmed with flaming hibiscus and other luxuriant tropical flowers. Janie, who had been flown up from school as a special surprise, rushed into her mother's arms for a hug, and then the room quieted down as everyone enjoyed the culinary delights provided for this very special evening. Fonduloha (exotic tropical fruit salad), spiced Bangkok chicken, and flavored rice gave the menu an international flair. There was much "oohing" and "ahing" over Janell Moore's lovely heart cake of three tiers with "We Love You, Wanda" on top. The evening was filled with nostalgia as the group watched films of the beginning of the work at Kudjip. The missionary kids sent their elders into waves of laughter as they gave their rendition of the "Delirious Doughnut," an original skit of Wanda's attempt to teach her cookboy how to make doughnuts. It was an evening of enjoying, loving, and being together in the "bond of love." It confirmed what Wanda had once said when asked why the Nazarene missionaries seemed to get along so well, while other mission staffs seemed to have strife. Wanda had replied, "It's because we have so many parties. We know how to love each other."

Wanda settled in to her new environment and faced her new challenges with the same indomitable spirit she had portrayed in the past. She did her best, but as Dr. Norman O. Miller expressed it, "Her heart was not here. Her first love was being a missionary, not an administrator." Wanda and Dr. Miller were to become fast friends, and she often sought his office as an oasis where she could let her hair down and just talk, mostly about spiritual things but also about issues that troubled her. Wanda felt very strongly about excessive promotion. She felt God's will was the ultimate influencing factor in promotion, not "moving up to the next level." She so strongly believed in working for achievement rather than recognition that she refused an honorary doctorate offered her.

Throughout the year, her schedule kept accelerating until in a letter to her friend Ginny she exclaimed, "I had a meeting at 9 A.M., one at lunch, one at 1:00, one at 3:45, one at 7:00, and got home about 11:15 P.M. Meetings started at 8:30 Saturday morning, and I got home that night about 10:30. I'm a little tired—and miles behind. No Christmas decorations up or anything. Believe I'll go back to New Guinea!" Not only was the office schedule busy, but also there was much traveling connected with her new job. Once she reported driving nearly 1,300 miles in less than a day and a half.

Though often exhausted, Wanda knew where to regain

her strength. Many times she would write notes similar to this: "I've lost two days' work in the office, but maybe it's been worth it. I was feeling the need of a break. I feel refreshed. I felt God's strength and help so much these two days." And afterward this inner strength would then overflow into her work, as when she wrote, "Meeting was good . . . free spirit of oneness, love . . . much business accomplished—prayer and fasting together—all in all, I'm pleased."

Because of Wanda's openness and directness, sometimes interpersonal relationships were strained, and feelings would get ruffled. Wanda fought for principles and, when she thought she was right, was determined to see right prevail. Sometimes that caused private pain. One day in the midst of a General NWMS Council meeting, she excused herself and called her dear friend, Kathy Butts, to meet her in the parking lot. In the car, she told Kathy to drive while she poured out her frustration in tears for several miles. When the storm passed, she wiped her eyes, turned Kathy back to Headquarters, and went back to the council meeting, and no one ever knew what happened. When people did disagree with Wanda, she always found it an occasion to do a careful introspection with the aid of the Holy Spirit to see if there were shortcomings within her that caused a negative influence in the situation. With that kind of an attitude, situations did turn around, and often Wanda was to write positive words such as this: "These are good days. I can't remember if I told you on the phone, but . . . have had excellent rapport . . . I feel God has given us a new freedom, and I praise Him for it. Council meeting should be good this year."

Wanda's five years in the NWMS office were marked

with notable accomplishments, but she was not looking for commendation. As she noted in her first report, "I look forward to this coming year with anticipation and will do my best to fulfill the responsibilities given me. I plan to talk with my Father rather often about it, for it's His 'Well done' that I openly covet." She began the quadrennium with the promise from Revelation 3, believing Christ was saying to the NWMS, "Behold, I have set before thee an open door, and no man can shut it: for thou hast a little strength, and hast kept my word, and hast not denied my name" (v. 8). Her promise to the General Board and general superintendents was, "It will be great to enter that door this quadrennium—for Him and with you."

At the end of the first year all the statistics had a plus, and during the next four years Wanda practiced fiscal responsibility by seeing that the NWMS department was in the black. During Wanda's administration, a new Mission Achievement Award program was introduced: NWMS membership (70% of church membership), books read (two times total NWMS members), and General Budget paid in full. LINKS was instigated, which was an expanded box work program of "adopting" the missionaries. Mission education was improved, with tapes of national music and testimonies added to the resource packet, as well as tapes developed for the visually handicapped. In 1978 a new tool for mission education was added with the inclusion of an NWMS Leadership CST (Christian Service Training) course. Alabaster boxes were redesigned, and Dr. Jerald D. Johnson noted in his 1980 report to the General Board that Alabaster giving increased by $200,000, "a gain which we believe the Alabaster toolboxes helped us to achieve. Greatest returns from the toolboxes occurred in those districts where the toolboxes were promoted through the Mission to the World rallies." New mission education tools were developed, and children's, youth, and adult packets containing many teaching aids were included with the year's lessons.

Children's interest in missions was a primary focus of Wanda's, and she tried several creative ways of developing that interest. In 1976 the NWMS sponsored a writing contest to encourage MKs to express some of their feelings about being MKs and to tell some of their experiences. Wanda compiled the stories of the winners, as well as honorable mentions, in a book titled *MKs Speak Up*. Stories with titles such as "Fire Walking," "Snakes Alive," "Only One Arm," "Scared Stiff," "Earthquake," "The Kid Killer," and Marlin Lathrop's first-place story of "Under Fire," an account of his experiences growing up in war-torn Beirut—these generated the same kind of missionary excitement Wanda had experienced in the attic missionary meetings many years before. Wanda's creativity and imagination also produced *The Mysterious Car* in 1979, a book dedicated to her own children and to all children who were traveling a road that God had marked out for each of them.

Of all emphases of the NWMS, Wanda was most concerned about prayer. She believed with full confidence that only as Prayer and Fasting is stressed, sought after, and held up as the foundation of all other areas would the church be able to see the success God wanted it to achieve. As she stated in her 1978 report to the General Board, "I read somewhere recently that the important task at hand is to link God's material gifts with the church's material needs. Well, I have a deep, burning desire that while we are busy about our task of 'linking God's material gifts with the church's material needs,' we will also be just as fervent and faithful in linking His spiritual gifts with her spiritual needs." In 1979 the General Council voted to make the year of 1979-80 a special year of Prayer, Fasting, and Self-denial; and in 1980 Wanda was able to report a growing emphasis on prayer. Many churches were beginning or re-organizing prayer groups, and local and district prayer retreats were being enthusiastically reported.

February 23, 1980, was a red-letter day for Wanda. As she explained it, "God spoke to me—clearly, as He always has in the past, when He was leading in a certain way. I felt that same inner assurance that I felt when going to Bethany, when getting married, when going to New Guinea the first and second time, and when coming back from New Guinea. He has released me from my responsibilities here at Headquarters. He told me clearly of one thing I must do first. I've done it and He took care of it. Now I must wait for His timing to talk to Dr. Jerry and Dr. Coulter. It's a good timing. I feel good about the future of the church. I feel at peace about many things. Where to from here? I'm not sure. I have felt 'nudges' but no clear direction from Him. I must have as much assurance that I am doing what He wants me to do as that I am leaving when He wants me to leave. It's been a transition time for NWMS and for me. I must leave 'results' with Him alone. That the God of the Universe cares enough to speak, to guide, to nudge—what more could we want!" Wanda admitted that the five years in Kansas City were rather hard on her, but she was there because she fully believed God had put her there, and she had done her best. Quoting Dr. T. W. Willingham, she would say, "Even an angel can't do better than his best." She readily admitted she had learned a lot.

When Wanda shared her "nudge" with Dr. Johnson, he

urged her to pray a little more and wait a few weeks. She did so but, feeling even more assured of God's leading, they together shared with the general superintendents, then the NWMS Council, and then openly. Wanda began to prepare to enter college after the General Convention in June to complete her degree before going to different areas of the world as a "supply" missionary.

One day, Dr. Johnson asked her if she'd like to go to Israel to replace the Morgans while they were on furlough. She could attend school in Israel. After checking in with her Heavenly Father, Wanda felt she was heading in the right direction and excitedly began making plans. After the General Assembly in June, where she would officially terminate her office, she would fly to Papua New Guinea for the 25th anniversary of the opening of the field and then on to Jerusalem. (In 1975 the Australian-administered territories of Papua and New Guinea combined to form the independent nation of Papua New Guinea.) At great peace, Wanda once again declared, "Wherever He leads is good enough for me. I want to be a channel—a vessel He can move and use in any way He wishes." And now to think, she would be walking the very paths where once her Lord had walked. This, she felt, was a cherished gift from God that she was to treasure to the end of her days.

An added benefit of Wanda's five years in Kansas City had been the opportunity to be near her children. She felt it was indeed in God's providence to be able to provide a home for them at this time. These young adult years of making adjustments to college, seeking a career, finding a life partner, becoming established spiritually were difficult ones. Wanda had always leaned heavily upon the Lord to guide her children, and she had accepted separation from them willingly to do His work; but she loved being near them during these years, for above all of her other titles and jobs, she loved being a mother.

5

Mother

JANIE, HER CHIN RESTING in her hands and her brows furrowed, yelled in to the next room, "Hey, Mother, how do you spell *discussion?*"

Wanda, with a chuckle, replied, "I don't spell it—I just like doing it."

"Amen," Janie fervently replied.

Such free give-and-take exchanges characterized the special relationship Wanda had with her children. Not having a father made Geron and Janie's relationship with their mother quite unique. Wanda diligently worked to fill that gap and assumed both the role of father and mother. However, she kept the children very aware of their dad. In a letter to Ginny Griffin she commented, "The kids are fine. They're anxious for Christmas Eve to get here. I enjoy them so much. We were going through some old pictures one night, and I gave Janie one of her daddy and me. She has carried it and hung on to it tenaciously since then." In another letter telling of Geron's success with the debate team, she remarked, "They came out first, winning a trophy for the school! I told Geron he was a chip off the old block . . . I still have Sid's debate letter he won in high school." Another time, she commented, after Geron had spoken in church, "Geron amazes me. He spoke in church last night, and his delivery was good, even if I do say so myself. Honestly, it made me so lonely for Sid, I could hardly stand it. He has a lot of his dad in him, that boy—even though he's never really been with him."

On the flyleaf of her diary, Wanda wrote, "To my kids, Geron Murray and Janie Marie, who have been such a delight to me through the years." Wanda truly delighted in her children. Janie remembers her mom reminding her and Geron that they were a joy to her at every stage, and after God, they came before anything. Janie acknowledges that declaration was not just mere rhetoric, but by her words and deeds, Wanda revealed her love and concern for her children. There were fantastic birthday parties, joyous Christmas celebrations, and so many special fun-packed activities.

One lonely night when Wanda was separated from family and friends, she wrote to her kids in her diary. She knew it might be years before they read it; but overcome with emotion and longing for them, she wrote, "I hope you know how much I enjoyed each of you. How I enjoyed sharing your activities: the sports days, cake auctions, Christmas parties at Banz, your school programs at Banz and then in Ukarumpa. How many times I thanked God

Janie, Wanda, and Geron

for giving you to me. How much you enriched my life. You were never far from my mind. When I shopped, I automatically looked for 'little things for Christmas stockings.' I liked to surprise you and always wanted the best for 'my kids.' I loved your friends and was always so proud of you, not for accomplishments, though you both had plenty of those, but just because you were good kids. You still are, and I still desire the best for you and now your families. I wish I could really open my heart and tell you how deeply I'm feeling all this tonight. Someday I'll be gone and can't tell you in person anymore, so I want to just remind you that the 'best' always will center in your commitment to Him. Go ahead—say, Mom has to preach!"

There were very open lines of communication between Wanda and the children, and Wanda loved to talk with her kids. Janie shared that growing up, she felt she probably put her mom on a pedestal because of Wanda's deep commitment to God and His work. However, as Janie grew older, she felt that her relationship with her mother changed, and really, Wanda became a dear friend as well as mother. She was able to share very deep feelings with her mom. Wanda remembered good sharing times when Janie was a teenager. She commented in a letter home, "I took off a couple of weekends ago to go see Janie in their school production of *Oklahoma*. It was cute, and they'd all worked so hard. Excuse my prejudiced view, but Janie looked like a doll. She insisted I sleep in her room, and we stayed awake a long time talking. She seemed so free in sharing things with me. I'm so grateful for this. She talks freely about any subject, and there seems to be no barriers. Actually, I'm surprised at her mature attitude toward most things. She has started looking for answers for herself in the Word. If she keeps this up, I have no fears for her future. She is very sensitive but levelheaded, and I feel a new bond. Isn't God good to us?" Again, in another letter Wanda reminisced, "Speaking of Geron coming home, he is a joy to my heart. I can tell a real difference in him. It was so much fun having him home. We discussed everything—he's just discovering his powers of conversation."

Wanda hated to be separated from her children, but when they reached high school age, they had to leave home to continue their education. Ukarumpa High School is operated by Wycliffe Bible Translators on their base in the Eastern Highlands. The Wycliffe organization welcomed the Church of the Nazarene to use the high school facilities. Nazarene Mission built a children's hostel there on the base, and a missionary couple was assigned to be mother and father to the dozen children residing there. Geron, in remembering those early separations, said, "Mom so trusted God for the care of her children that we felt totally loved but released to be free—no overprotection. She didn't worry about us. Had she been overprotective, she'd never been able to be as committed to her work as she was." Years later, Geron marveled at this attitude of his mom when his own child was born. "I didn't realize the depth of Mom's commitment until I wanted to surround my little girl with protective boundaries so that she wouldn't get hurt. But Mother did not place them about us. She completely entrusted us to God's care."

Wanda was very grateful for Ukarumpa. "I am so happy Geron can be in this high school," she wrote home. "While I was there, they announced the names of the boy and girl who had the highest grade point average of the semester. Geron was the boy, so needless to say I was rather happy about it. Oh, that doesn't mean he's very smart. It's only a small school, but it does mean he's well-adjusted and trying to do his best, and he has Christian fellowship on top of it. What more could you ask for your kids?"

The separation was hard, and often Wanda commented how much she and Janie missed Geron. However, Wanda found creative ways to keep in touch. One Easter when he wasn't able to come home, she and Janie took five other teenagers on the station and flew to see him. Wanda cooked for 12 for four days. She exclaimed, "That's a job! It was so good to see Geron. He's really a young man now. He made first string on the basketball team, he's taking trombone lessons, and he is choir manager. He's involved —and loves it. I'm so proud of him—that 'mother heart,' you know, and soon Janie will be a teenager."

And soon Janie was ready to go to Ukarumpa as well. It was at this time that Geron also traveled back to the States to attend MidAmerica Nazarene College. Wanda faced lonely hours. She wrote, "Have heard several times from Geron now. I sure miss that boy. And yesterday Janie went off to school. So the house seems extra empty. How come they grow up so quickly?"

In a later letter she wrote, "We had a nice Christmas but different than any before. Of course, we didn't have Geron, so we invited five of the single girls over for dinner to open gifts, listen to 'Amahl,' and spend the night. We got to bed about 4 A.M. and were back up at 6:30 A.M. We had Christmas Day services and dinner together as a missionary family. Then 22 people came over to my house for games. We had Scrabble, Password, Yahtzee, etc., as we nibbled nuts and cookies and drank coffee and coffee and coffee! My large coffee urn Geron gave me last year came in real handy! It was all fun, but I still missed Geron!"

Time passed swiftly by, and Wanda was busily shopping for Janie's first formal to wear at her senior banquet, and it was time for Janie to leave for the States. In God's timing, Wanda prepared to leave the field and take up her assignment in Kansas City. Going home with Janie allayed some of the fears Wanda had about her children's adjustment to American culture. She wrote thanking Ginny Griffin for a package sent to Janie, "Janie was delighted with both the Bible and the shoes and especially the Bible. It was just what she wanted, and she reads it faithfully. She's a very conscientious Christian. I hope she stays that way when we come to the States. It's funny, but the States will probably be more of an adjustment to my two teenagers than the New Guinea field was to me when I first came out. (I was only 24 so not much more than a teenager!) Anyway, if they'll just keep Christ first, they won't have any problem."

Wanda had a deep concern for young people, not only her own children but also those she came in contact with on the mission field and in the States. In a letter home she mentioned a record Geron had that had a song that haunted her. It was called "Shades of Gray." Wanda urged, "Listen to it sometimes, and it will hurt you to see how confused our young people feel. They need a strong faith in God—a sense of purpose more than ever before."

Janie and Geron admit that their mother had a very forceful personality, sometimes almost domineering. She voiced her opinions freely. Janie says she never questioned or talked back when she was young. She received few spankings, for she melted into tears when her mother looked crossly at her. Geron voiced his opinions more, which led to some heart-to-heart talks between mother and son. However, Janie says that now she realizes that what her mother was molded her own personality in such a way that as an adult she feels much freer to voice her opinions.

The greatest tribute to Wanda from her kids was as Janie expressed it, "Everything she said to us, everything she told us, everything she believed, she lived. Her total commitment to Christ was amazing. I have never met anyone so concerned with following God. She was so open, so vibrant. She automatically talked about the Lord. Sometimes it made us kids cringe, but she was so natural. You don't see that single-mindedness, that total submission to

God's will a lot today, even among Christians."

One Mother's Day, Janie penned a tribute to Wanda that expresses the legacy of love given by Wanda to her children. She had been hailed as a pioneer missionary, an outstanding teacher, an effective administrator, and an eloquent speaker, but no title pleased her more than "Beloved Mother."

A Tribute to My Mother

Mother,
On this special day—your day—
I simply wish to tell you all the
Things I've felt inside
About you being my mother.
The past few years have become a
Gift to me from the Lord, because I feel
That in that time I have
Come to realize and understand how precious
The bond between a mother and
Daughter can be.
Mom,
You gave me so much—
A lot of things that I needed,
Yet so many more that I didn't but
That make life very pleasant.
I am truly grateful for them all.
But mostly for the home
You gave me . . .
Because it is out of that home where I received love;
And that love has seen me through
Lots of tears and doubts;
Through anxieties that weren't always real.

It has listened to little heartbreaks, and
—counseled in times of need,
—given time to accounts of endless tales,
—rejoiced when I have been successful,
—sorrowed when I have been hurting,
And it has given
So much more than it has taken!
You were more than a mother to me.
You were my friend, and you showed me
What Christ can do
With a person who is doing only
What *He* wants.
The riches I received when I was home were not
The material ones, but the
Intangible ones that are hidden deep within me;
Ones that I shall hold
On to forever.
You touched and will continue to touch
So many lives without having to have
Ever spoken in a
Crowded auditorium—
In a world that is unfortunately full of untruthfulness,
You were total honesty.
I guess that is why you appealed
To young people.
You lived what you spoke about.
If my son looks at me only a portion of the way I
Always saw you,
I will feel blessed.
You have challenged me to be the best mother I
Possibly can,
But more importantly, to give to my children

The one gift
We all can give them . . .
That of instilling in them the desire to be
Only
What God
Wants them to be.
All mothers can be truly special—
I'm so glad you were mine!
JANIE (KNOX) NORRICK

Wanda's love for children overflowed beyond her own, and she became a favorite missionary aunt to many missionary children all over the world. Aunt Wanda endeared herself to children and teens who needed a listening ear and an understanding heart. Her door was always open, and so was her heart.

6

Aunt Wanda

RAIN POUNDED on the metal roof and fell in blinding sheets, driving everyone inside. However, the group of teens and children sprawled in front of the brightly blazing hearth and sampling the delicious glazed doughnuts freshly made in Wanda's kitchen seemed blissfully oblivious to the storm. Any excuse was a good one to come visit Aunt Wanda. The Blowers and Eby children secretly hoped that the storm would continue and that maybe the mountain road would be impassable and their folks would decide to spend the night. Aunt Wanda's house was often a refuge in such circumstances. To be able to play games, to sing, to eat one of her delicious meals, to just be around Aunt Wanda afforded these missionary kids and their parents a delightful experience.

A love for children had been an outstanding characteristic of both Sid and Wanda's personalities. Someone asked Wanda once what she considered Sid's greatest weakness. That was a tough question, for it was difficult for Wanda to equate weakness with Sidney at all. After thinking a moment, she had responded, "He really loved children, and the children loved him. I can see him now standing at the door greeting people, with children jumping at his knees." She seemed to be defining weakness as being softhearted and compassionate to children, and if so, she was the same. However, instead of weakness, it proved to be one of the greatest strengths of her life. Her love for her own children encompassed all the others that came into her life.

"Aunt Wanda" became the substitute for all the stateside family relationships of many a missionary child. It was not that they didn't care for their relatives, but they were thousands of miles away, and Aunt Wanda was right there for them—generous, loving, encouraging, supporting—helping them to love each other and to know and love God. As Linda (Bolerjack) Mealiff said, "I never thought of calling Aunt Wanda anything but that. She always was and always will be 'Aunt Wanda' to me. Other missionaries came and went and were 'Aunt' or 'Uncle' for a time, but they are not that to me anymore, but Aunt Wanda will always remain that to me. My husband and my children, who never even knew her in New Guinea, call her that too, for she left such an impact on all of our lives."

Younger children loved the seemingly endless supply of treats they found at Wanda's house, particularly candy and bubble gum from America. Birthday and Christmas gifts were always special, and many an MK was introduced to C. S. Lewis through *The Chronicles of Narnia* and Tolkein through *The Hobbit* and *Lord of the Rings* as libraries and minds were enriched. Youngsters often camped out at her house to read her collection of Peanuts comic books. She seemed to have all that were ever written. Darlene (Blowers) Brooks said even to this day when she sees Charlie Brown, she thinks of Aunt Wanda. Wanda always seemed to have time for each child and made each one feel special and loved.

Christmas was just more special because of Wanda's influence and participation. The Christmas season opened in New Guinea on December 1 with a plate of fresh doughnuts from Wanda's kitchen delivered to each missionary home. She decorated her house then, and most of the other families followed her example. From then on, Christmas was truly in the air, and the children's anticipation rose to a feverish pitch. Though she was very busy with programs at both school and church, she also encouraged the MKs to put on Christmas dramas for the English service and prepare skits and poems and songs for the traditional Christmas missionary dinner. Wanda would have friends in the States send special goodies for Christmas to add to the missionary family celebration. She always seemed to be able to find fireworks and sparklers to make the celebration a truly festive occasion. Writing to Ginny Griffin, Wanda once commented, "Ebys just came back from furlough, and they said their kids didn't enjoy Christmas in the States nearly as much as they do here in New Guinea. When I asked why, Carol said she thought it must have been because there was so much there. The stores were so loaded with toys and candy and goodies, until it took the edge off for them. While over here, every small thing seems to mean quite a lot. I think she may have a point." Because the

Wanda sharing the fun at a party

Knoxes were so well known, they always received more cards and gifts than anyone else, but Wanda was so generous with their abundance that the other children were kept from being envious. To missionary kids, Christmas and Aunt Wanda will always go together as an inseparable memory.

Wanda also had a great interest in MK teens. She seemed to be always doing something with them or for them. For most of the teenage MKs growing up in the 1960s at Kudjip, Wanda was their social hub. Linda (Bolerjack) Mealiff said that, as an eight-year-old in 1963 when she first met Wanda, she knew this lady was already a heroine in the church. She'd read about her in her junior missionary books, but though Wanda was so renowned, she was approachable. At that time, the teens were on correspondence studies, and sport and social opportunities with other teens were very limited. Wanda made sure their days were filled with good, wholesome, fun-filled activities. Wanda knew how to have fun. Steve White remembers one morning when they had gathered for school. Instead of the usual pep talk and devotions, Wanda told the teens to go home, get their towels and swimsuits, and meet back at her house. She then took them all in a Missionary Aviation Fellowship chartered plane to Madang, about a hundred miles away, to swim for the day and celebrate Geron's birthday. What a special birthday party that turned out to be!

She encouraged them to make music together. Among the Bolerjack, Eby, White, Blowers, Garner, and Powers teens and her own children, Geron and Janie, there were budding musicians of the guitar, piano, brass, and voice, and many an hour was spent in practicing, playing, and recording. She patiently recorded them on reel-to-reel tapes and made them feel very professional. Often she would take them to the Christian Leadership Training College across the valley where her friend, Geoff Baskett, would let them record in his radio studio, and then the Kudjip Teen Beats would feel they really were making it big-time.

Every Saturday on Kudjip station, all the tennis fans seemed to come out of hiding and meet at the tennis court for an afternoon of fun and fellowship. Wanda was always there raring to go, and it would not have been the same without her. She encouraged the teens to play, as well as the adults, and especially the girls, for she thought tennis was a good sport for girls as they could obtain good exercise, expertise, and skill, and still be ladies.

In the early days before the teens went away to high

school, Wanda supervised their correspondence studies. One of the original classroom buildings that was no longer used by the elementary school was set up as a mini high school for about 10 teens who were ready for high school curriculum. Each teen had his own individual desk and course, and Wanda supervised. She provided a stimulating learning environment but also demanded the best of the students. She would not let them slide by or be mediocre if they could achieve at a higher level. As Dave Blowers remembers, "Even when she was stern, I did not feel less accepted." Steve White remembers that Wanda would occasionally leave the classroom to go to her house, and when she returned would often place a glass of crushed ice on his desk as she passed him on her way to her desk. She liked to chew ice and knew Steve did too. It was such a simple gesture but just another way to say, "You're special, and I care." Steve remembers that Wanda encouraged the teens to create a yearbook in 1965 for their mini high school; it turned out to be so much fun, and it is one of his special keepsakes today.

Wanda had a knack for making people feel special. Dave Blowers also shared that the conversations they had together "that were ours were very significant. Though I frequently felt awkward in groups of people, I do not recall ever feeling awkward toward Aunt Wanda." Dave remembers two aspects of Wanda's life that then and now have exerted a great influence on his life. "She seemed to be, in a very natural way, disarmingly generous; and she combined generosity with a festive and joyful spirit that was very engaging to me." He found it unusual to find a festive "people person" who also was intellectually astute. Though, as Dave said, "she would probably shudder at that phrase, she modeled for me a life in which the intellect was shown not only to be compatible with faith but a great asset to it as well. The combination of a festive spirit with a vigorous mind is what I found to be so admirable about Aunt Wanda."

Wanda was a great encourager to many a youngster who was working through problems of adjustment to the mission field in a new environment and culture. Very concerned about one young man who seemed so introverted and shy, she asked him to her house one evening as her special guest. She cooked his favorite food, and then they spent the evening in front of the fireplace in intense concentration over the chess board. She had also bought him a stamp book, so they worked on stamps together. Wanda attempted to keep conversation going with little success. Finally, at the close of the evening, because of a sudden downpour she took him home in the car, though it was just the other side of the station. Feeling a bit downhearted at what she felt was not a very successful evening of heart-to-heart conversation, she let him out at his front door. He hadn't said a word all the way home, but when Wanda stopped the car, he grabbed her around the neck and kissed her. Then he jumped out and ran inside. Wanda said, "I nearly cried." Surprised and elated, she drove home feeling much more encouraged and determined to try to spend more time with this teen, though her spare time was very limited. Future days proved the good accomplished on that special evening.

Mark Eby remembers the years of discussing philosophy and literature with Wanda face-to-face, then by letter. Remembering, Mark said, "I had personally identified with a character named Asher Lev created by a Jewish author,

Chaim Potak. Asher Lev was a gifted young artist in an orthodox Jewish home where making a graven image was heresy. His was an emotional and intellectual rebellion against the spiritually confining structure of his religion. Aunt Wanda acknowledged my struggle, but she wrote to me lovingly about the 'lighthearted sense of fun' that I seemed to have misplaced somewhere." Wanda had reminded Mark that everything is not so "life-and-death seriousness." She had said, "There's a playfulness about life that I believe is God-intended." Mark concluded, "Aunt Wanda had dealt with life-and-death seriousness and had rejected cynicism as an option. I have learned to do the same, but it is not based on frivolousness or blind hope. It has taken a lifetime of thinking through the incongruities of our faith to arrive at 'playfulness.' It is my gift from Aunt Wanda."

While Wanda was serving as NWMS executive director in Kansas City, her home in Olathe, Kans., which was only a stone's throw from the campus of MidAmerica Nazarene College, became an oasis to MK college students and their buddies. To many it seemed a "branch office of Papua New Guinea." It was a way to keep in touch with the home country. Wanda allowed the college students to use her home as a place to escape the monotony of dorm life and campus food. As the students faced important decisions in their lives, she was the one who became a sounding board and was asked for her insights and advice. She substituted for missionary parents many times. Linda (Bolerjack) Mealiff shared that it was at Aunt Wanda's at a Thanksgiving dinner that she and Dave, now her husband, recognized that "electricity" between them as more than just friendship.

Wanda had a special way of including the MKs' friends who had not grown up on the mission field, and she became "Aunt Wanda" to them as well. With many of these newcomers to the PNG extended family, she had lively discussions about God's Word. Someone commented during a Sunday dinner clean-up session time, "Aunt Wanda seems to be having a good time." Janie agreed and said, "Yes, she's doing what she likes to do best, and that's talk about the Lord." On more than one occasion, Wanda would take a volume of C. S. Lewis from the bookshelf to read a passage that shed light on the conversation at hand. Darlene (Blowers) Brooks said Wanda seemed to have every book ever written by C. S. Lewis. In college and in later years as Darlene read C. S. Lewis's writings, she said she understood why Wanda thought so much of him, although she never claimed to understand him as Wanda did. However, she was very grateful for Wanda's insights and the intellectual views she shared.

Wanda was a very careful thinker. Dave Blowers remembers that once with a twinkle in her eye, she asked him to explain a careless platitude he had foolishly tried to pass off as profound. He was surprised and challenged that an adult outside of his immediate family would take his words so seriously. As a psychology major, Mary Jo Bolerjack said that it bothered her at first that Wanda was so dogmatically antipsychologist. Wanda felt people ran too quickly to man for answers rather than going to God. However, Mary Jo commented, "Now, after gaining a few years of observing people and developing my own relationship with God, I think she had a good point. Most people don't really know or believe in how much God cares about all our dilemmas and confusion."

Mary Jo also remembers a time she attended a banquet at which Wanda was the speaker. Wanda was introduced as a fine, dedicated Christian woman who never even questioned God or His calling on her life. When Wanda got up to speak, she made it immediately clear that she had questioned God many times over many issues. But that's how she had built such a strong faith. She had allowed Him to show her how much He cared, and she had learned how He could handle all kinds of disappointments, questions, and tragedies of life.

As many MKs reminisced and recaptured memories of Aunt Wanda, they agreed that it seemed as if Wanda was always having fun, never working—but then they concluded that her work was her fun, her joy in serving God. There was no compartmentalizing her service to God. Darlene (Blowers) Brooks says, "The song 'O to Be like Thee' always reminds me of Aunt Wanda. . . . I could tell she meant and lived the words of that song. I shall be forever indebted to her for her example of Christ to me. I consider her as one of my role models of the kind of Christian I want to be." That declaration could be repeated by dozens of missionary kids who felt the influence of Wanda Knox's life. Wanda will live on in the hearts of those around the world who were privileged to know her as "Aunt Wanda."

7

Beloved Friend

THE STILLNESS of the evening was broken by the quiet strumming of a guitar. A full moon bathed the mission station in beautiful shimmering light, most lights were out, and everyone was settling to sleep. Everyone, that is, but Wanda and her housemate, Jan Watson, who were sitting on the front steps, relaxing in the beautiful, peaceful atmosphere of the tropical night. For Wanda, life seemed to begin at 10 P.M., though she would often be up again at 6 A.M. running her tennis racket along the wall of Nancy Seale's bedroom as she walked by, hoping to find an early tennis partner. Many of her partners can remember her taking blankets with her to wipe up the early morning dew on the grass courts. Wanda believed playing together was a good way to learn to know someone. She was glad she lived on the mission field, where she could follow that philosophy. She sometimes found it difficult to find time in America just to relax and once complained to a furloughing missionary, "I'm anxious to get home. They don't know how to play here!"

At home, at school, at church, in the office—wherever Wanda went—she was surrounded by those who called her "friend." She had the unique ability to make a special friend of every person who came into her life in more than just a brief, casual encounter. She made the individual feel so important and so gave herself that each one felt Wanda was his best friend. A favorite phrase of hers was Ralph Waldo Emerson's "My friends have come to me unsought. The great God gave them to me." Wanda considered friends a very special gift from God. In a letter to Ginny Griffin, Wanda expressed it this way: "There is a special spot—special place in our heart and life that a certain friend fills that no one else can fill—though they have their special place too. Nice." Quoting one of her school friends, Freda Rhodes, Wanda said, "She once said that the older she grew, the more she realized the best beauty was found in the lives of her friends. I kinda agree." Wanda early began to seek that beauty.

Wanda met Ginny Griffin in Bethany Nazarene College, and though they were friends there, a much deeper relationship was formed as they corresponded through the years while Wanda was on the mission field and as she lived and traveled in the U.S. Sitting on a plane or in a terminal, she would dash a note to Ginny. Her unique salutations of "Hi Outfit," "Critter," or "Hootenanny" became special. Ginny has been able to share memories of Wanda in a special way from her collection of correspondence dating back to 1960. To Ginny and many others, she loved to send cards, often Peanuts cards, and would underline significant words and expressions or add her own between the lines. She loved to discuss the Bible in her letters, and often she and Ginny would select portions of Scripture to read "together," though thousands of miles apart. Then they would discuss them for weeks through their letters. Wanda also loved to share good books. She was an avid reader and shared the insights and inspiration she received. She also loved to debate the issues she read about. Nancy Seale remembers that often Wanda would be reading in bed at 11 P.M. and would call out to her roommates, "Hey! listen to this."

Ginny often did stateside shopping for Wanda, sending her goodies and items unobtainable in New Guinea. Once after receiving an especially lovely parcel, Wanda, overwhelmed, wrote Ginny: "Oh, me, when you do things, you really do them up in a big way. We do appreciate them so much, but I do feel you have sent too much. I shall just quote you a little saying on friendship for future reference! Ha. 'We do not wish for friends to clothe and feed our body but to do the like office for our spirit.' I can't remember who wrote that, but I like it. And, Ginny, you do pretty well at the clothing and feeding the spirit. Anyway, thanks for your very generous gifts and for your love."

Wanda formed some very strong bonds of friendship among many of the New Guinea people, and one of the very first was Meri (Mary) Tultul (TOOL-tool) of the De-monka (duh-MONK-kuh) tribe. Meri is the pidgin word for woman, and tultul was the name given to the leader of a tribe. This woman's husband had been the Demonka tultul. When he died, she took his place as the tribe's representative to the government. This was very unusual in this male-dominated society, but Meri Tultul had unusual poise and ability. She was referred to as the "Queen." She and Wanda had an unusual rapport, and to Wanda's joy, Meri Tultul became the first Christian from the Kurumul church. She influenced her community for God and the church. It was a great loss to the community and to Wanda when Meri Tultul lost her life in an accidental drowning.

Another close friend of Wanda's was Amb (AHMP) Tur (TOUR), a 4 feet 6 inch spiritual giant. She considered herself Wanda's mother in the Lord and would often slip in Wanda's back door, always with a gift, and drop on her knees to pray. Many times if caught by a tropical storm or approaching darkness, she would spend the night on Wanda's front veranda on a cozy pallet especially reserved for her. Beds were too high above the floor for her liking. She knew her special spot was always available whenever she needed it.

Poundakuk (POUND-a-cook) was a lady Wanda met on the road as she motorbiked to one of the outstation churches. Wanda invited her to church, where she found Christ as her own personal Savior. Because she considered Wanda her spiritual mother, a very close bond was formed. They were both devastated when Poundakuk was diagnosed with terminal cancer. Carolyn (Parsons) Hannay remembers that her first week on the mission field she was privileged to go with Wanda and Dr. Glenn Irwin to make a home visit to Poundakuk. The doctor was going to change Poundakuk's dressings. Carolyn reminisced, "As we approached the house, I saw the wee grass hut nestled in a beautiful setting of banana trees. Flowers lined the narrow pathway up the home. Inside, the petite old woman lay on a straw mat. The odor from the dirty bandage was almost unbearable. As Dr. Irwin changed the dressing, Wanda visited and prayed with her friend. Poundakuk cried with joy when she saw Wanda coming up the path and thanked her over and over again for coming to visit her. I knew I had had a glimpse into the life of a great missionary lady. She had led this woman to Jesus, had taken her car over unpaved, rough roads to provide comfort and compassion, and done it all so unselfishly." Later through the months of hospitalization, Wanda daily visited Poundakuk, brought her food, prayed with her, and tried to make her last days as peaceful as possible, but Poundakuk seemed convulsed with fear. Finally, Wanda discovered Poundakuk's main fear. She knew the road to Minj and the road to Banz, but which was the road to heaven? So young in the faith and so steeped in the animistic fear of the ancestral spirits, she needed assurance of God's care and grace. Wanda was able to allay Poundakuk's fears and assure her that God would be with her in the valley of the shadow of death and that He would surely lead her onto the right road. Too weak to leave the hospital but desiring to be baptized, Poundakuk was sprinkled in her bed, and at last she was at peace.

In 1960 when Wanda returned to New Guinea after Sidney's death, she and the Whites became fast friends. Mona White speaks of their relationship: "We became very close. Wanda was like a real sister to both of us. She and Wallace called each other 'Doc.' We had lots of coffee breaks, tea breaks, mail from home breaks, laughs and tears, long jungle bush walks, and late, late nights of games such as Scrabble." The children of both families became very close as well. In a letter to the Whites while they were on furlough in 1964, Wanda was commenting on a snapshot the Whites had sent and said, "Robbie looked like he might have put on a little weight, and Steve? Well, like Geron said the very minute he looked at the picture (with love dripping from his tone), 'He's just the same old Steve!' Oh me, Isn't God good to us. I read somewhere recently that 'the highest bliss is communion of spirit with spirit; the deepest woe, the separation of friend from friend.' I sometimes think that life would be easier if we didn't have the capacity to feel so deeply, but then, it wouldn't mean as much either."

Through the next 15 years, many more missionaries would find Wanda a special friend. She held a unique position in the missionary family. She was a respected colleague of the men, as well as a very competitive chess and tennis partner. Darlene (Blowers) Brooks remembers her dad, Bruce, and Wanda spending hours over the chess board with occasional outbursts of laughter and, no matter who won, ending in good spirits with wonderful theological discussions interspersed with the chess plays. Ray Bolerjack remembers enjoying many a good game of tennis with Wanda. He also was often her rescuer on Sunday afternoons when muddy roads or flat tires delayed her return from Sunday services. Wanda was able to relate to the married women on staff in their roles of wives and mothers. Many a missionary mom knocked on Wanda's door and was welcomed in for a cup of coffee and a heart-to-heart chat, sharing burdens and joys. Wanda was also able to find excellent rapport with the single missionaries and understand their particular needs and problems. Friday evening suppers and game nights at Wanda's after a hard week's work were eagerly anticipated. When it was possible to leave the Highlands for a holiday, many of the singles would try to correlate their holiday time, and then they along with Wanda would travel to the coast for very enjoyable vacations. Wanda described one such holiday in a letter home: "We drove from here to Lae [350 miles], and Marjorie [Merritts] and Merna [Blowers] were with Janie and me. We were doing something all the time. We shopped, had picnics, went swimming, ate Chinese food, played games, etc. It was oodles of fun."

Wanda was also a favorite visitor to the mission outstations. She was a special "Auntie" to John Bromley and a very welcomed guest to the Bromley home in the Jimi Valley. She was a great comfort to Margaret Bromley in the years following Will's death. Visiting the Daryl Schendel family in the isolated Kopon (KO-bone) area was also delightful, but visiting the Kopon in the early days presented a real challenge, for there was a 13-mile walk in from the airstrip. Wanda decided to take up jogging to get in shape for the long trek. She selected the airstrip on Kudjip Station as her track. Helen Bolerjack remembers with a smile Wanda driving to the airstrip to get her exercise. Wanda reported her progress to Mona White: "I've taken up jogging. My first attempt was one mile in 11 minutes. Rather slow, I'm afraid—will see how much I can improve on that in the following weeks. A run up and down the airstrip in the cool of the evening is rather invigorating." Wanda's jogging highly amused the New Guineans. When she first started, people would call out, "Miss Wanda, Yu go we?" (You go where?) She'd reply, "Mi no save [SAH-veh], Mi ran [RON] nating tasol." (I don't know, I run nowhere.) Then they would yodel at her and have a big laugh.

Wanda's circle of friends extended beyond the missionary staff. There were many expatriates in the community who also became very special friends. Shortly after Wanda returned to New Guinea in 1960, she met a young German planter who managed a plantation near Kudjip. Jack Strohben, returning from a trip to the coast, was stranded in Banz without transport. He dropped in to the European Club, and someone mentioned that a lady missionary from Kudjip was in town and might give him a ride on her way home. Jack, clutching a bouquet of artificial flowers he'd brought from Madang, went in search of the lady and found Wanda. She graciously complied to his request but was curious as to why in this tropical paradise he would be bringing artificial flowers home. She mentioned she didn't like artificial flowers, and he assured her he'd grow real ones if he had them. She offered to share slips from her garden, and a friendship was in bloom. Three years later after a visit to Germany, Jack came home engaged to be married. His fiancée needed a place to stay until the wedding, and Wanda took Erika in with open arms. Erika could speak neither English nor pidgin, but she and Wanda smiled a lot until they could communicate in words.

The Strohbens lived at the plantation beside Kudjip until 1968. They were often at Wanda's for one of her delicious meals and an invigorating game of tennis or chess. Jack was one of Wanda's chess partners to whom she didn't like to lose. Jack remembers that whenever he got her into a corner, she would go to the fridge and get a glass of ice cubes and return to sit and crunch them, knowing Jack would be distracted and his concentration on the game broken. Most of the time she succeeded! Jack called Wanda "Sis" because she became like a real sister to him. She became "Tante Wanda" (aunt in German) to Jack and Erika's children and was a great comfort to the whole family when the oldest son tragically drowned in a pond near their home. The Strohbens moved in 1968 to the Eastern Highlands, and Wanda often visited them while on holiday. When they left the Kudjip area, they gave Wanda their horse and their dog for her to always have something to remember them by. Later they moved to Australia but kept in close contact. Jack commented that Wanda never forgot any of their birthdays. Wanda was able to visit the Strohbens in Australia as she traveled back to the U.S. Jack was not a believer but respected Wanda greatly for her beliefs. They would have lengthy discussions about religion and politics, and both felt free to state their individual opinions without having to convince each other. Out of it all a great friendship was forged, which, as Jack said, is "what life is all about."

Wanda's adjustment to Kansas City and a life-style much different from the mission field was made easier by some special relationships she formed with new friends. On a Christian Life/NWMS regional tour, Wanda and Donna Fillmore discovered a mutual love for Scrabble. In spite of the exhausting schedule, they would sit up late and play, and Donna remembers one night they were both so tired they could only think of three-letter words! Following the tour, Wanda dropped Donna a note, saying: "Have enjoyed getting to know you more on this trip. I have always enjoyed sitting on committees with you—admired your ability in children's writing—but now, I feel I know you more as a person. . . . I feel it a real privilege to share with you in a type of 'prayer fellowship' during these difficult days of adjustment. . . . Thanks again, just for being you." Wanda and Donna began meeting once a week for breakfast and became fast friends. Donna remembers that, when

Wanda was preparing to go to Israel, she knew Donna was to have surgery. So she planned ahead and ordered flowers to be waiting for Donna when she returned to the room.

Joyce Deasley remembers Wanda as the one who helped her and her family settle in to Kansas City. Wanda introduced them to all kinds of interesting restaurants and made herself available in various ways to make them feel at home. She became a frequent visitor at the Deasleys when she discovered Joyce made oatmeal porridge. With a cheerful, happy countenance, she would appear at 7 A.M., knock on the door, and say, "I've come for oatmeal." Joyce would eagerly invite her in for more than oatmeal; she knew a good time of fellowship and interaction was also on the menu. Joyce viewed Wanda as a marvelous debater, who never shied from any issue but never let the debate interfere with friendship. She observed Wanda as a tremendous listener and complimented her on not being a "top drawer person." Wanda was well aware of her churchwide prominence but never used it but rather was responsible to it. In spite of Wanda's busy schedule, she called Joyce weekly. They were a mutual encouragement to one another, and Wanda's unlimited faith had a special impact on Joyce's life. Joyce commented, "Wanda believed God is the answer to any problem, and she more than said it; she lived it. She was a real prayer warrior. I felt the communication line was a lot shorter between her and the Lord."

Kathy Butts and Wanda met in a rather unique way. Kathy did not know Wanda before Wanda accepted the position of NWMS executive director. However, after Wanda's first day, Kathy had a strange dream about Wanda and formed a rather negative opinion of her. When Kathy shared her dream with Esther McNutt, Esther exclaimed,

"Oh, Wanda is not like that at all! You've got to meet her. Come, we're going to have lunch." That luncheon began a friendship that was to grow and flourish in the days ahead.

Wanda had a great zest for life. She believed life was to be lived, and she lived it to the fullest. Helen Bolerjack, tongue in cheek, once remarked, "Wanda, you'll be alive until your last breath!" And Helen concluded, "I think she was." Kathy shared in many of those "living" experiences. Often Wanda would call Kathy up and say, "Let's get away for the weekend. I have a circular to look at property, and we can get something free." It didn't matter if it was a camera, tennis rackets, or set of knives, it was always an adventure for Wanda. On one such outing, they went to Lake Chapparal, where Wanda fell in love with a piece of property that reminded her of New Guinea. She bought it and named it Amamas (ah-ma-MOS), which means happiness in pidgin. Wanda set up a trailer on the property, and it became a favorite spot.

Wanda had a certain quality of naïveté but was able to laugh at herself. Kathy often called her "Calamity Jane," especially after the incident of the grapefruit. Kathy, just returning from a Florida vacation, offered Wanda a few grapefruit. Wanda dropped them into her bag and left for home. On the way, she decided to stop at the grocery store to pick up a few items. When she reached the checkout counter, she opened her purse to find she had neither money nor checkbook, but she did have two grapefruit, which aroused the cashier's suspicions. The cashier called the manager, and Wanda had to go back to the fruit counter to show she was not shoplifting. She explained the whole situation and even talked the manager into letting her take the groceries home and return with the money. A bag boy helped her out with the groceries, and then she discovered she had no car keys either. She suspected she'd dropped them on the pavement. The manager had followed them out, so she, the manager, and the bag boy all dropped to their knees in search of the keys! They were found, and at last she got home.

Kathy was usually Wanda's chauffeur to the airport when Wanda went out of town for speaking engagements. When she held missionary services, she usually carried all of her equipment. Kathy helped her haul the tape recorders, projector, and sound equipment to the plane and saw her safely on. However, Wanda once had to change planes in Chicago; and, overwhelmed with her heavy equipment, she flagged down a passing porter, who was going by with an empty wheelchair. She wanted to pile the equipment in and wheel it to her next plane. He suggested she just climb in and hold the equipment, and he would wheel her to the gate. She gratefully followed his suggestion. Evidently some of the other passengers saw her arrive in the chair, for after boarding the plane and reaching her next destination, the young man beside her said he'd be happy to assist her in deplaning. He thought she was handicapped!

Wanda touched hundreds of lives, and many of them called her "friend." Joyce Deasley wrote a special tribute in memory of her friendship with Wanda. It represents many others who would echo the same sentiment:

Thank You, Lord, for Wanda,
For all the heartwarming memories of special times
    together.
All of our times together have been special times.
I wouldn't want to find someone to take her place;

There's no one that could ever do that.
I've been busy with others,
Getting interested and involved,
Sometimes almost thinking of them as replacements;
But because my interactions with one individual are quite
     different from another's,
This makes our relationship one of a kind—
His, rich and rewarding.
I thank God for the privilege of friendship,
For the ability to remember all the parts that have been
     interwoven
To create a lasting handiwork of His created beauty
Through friendship.

8

Missionary to the World

IN THE SOUTH PACIFIC, the island of New Guinea hovers just above Australia like an ancient prehistoric bird settling down on its nest. The western side of the island is politically part of Indonesia and is named Irian Jaya. The eastern half is now the country of Papua New Guinea. Wanda, looking down at the mix of thick jungle inland and the congestion of streets and modern buildings bordering the coast, felt her mixed emotions as she approached Papua New Guinea soil once more. The jet maneuvered into its landing pattern, and soon Wanda deplaned and made her way into the airport terminal. This arrival was so different from the previous ones. This time she was alone—no husband and no children. This time she was not beginning a missionary term but making a brief stop on her way to

Israel and a missionary assignment there. She had 10 days to renew friendships, celebrate the 25th anniversary of the Nazarene work in Papua New Guinea, and rejoice at what had been accomplished for God and His kingdom. Anniversaries are reflections of beginnings, and the next 10 days were to be praise-filled hours for Wanda as she viewed the progress of the church in this land that had become "home" in such a special way to her.

As Wanda moved from place to place during those days, memories flooded her mind. On this very special occasion of the 25th anniversary, the new district center at Kiam (KEY-ahm) was dedicated. As Wanda sat in the service, she jotted down her reminiscences. She remembered when Sid and she had no Christian New Guinean friends with whom to find fellowship, and now here were hundreds and hundreds (almost a thousand) gathered singing God's praise. She rejoiced over the many pastors and their families present whom she had taught in grade school. She remembered when even a simple melody was difficult for the people to follow, and now here was a choir singing in four-part harmony! She remembered when missionaries had to do everything, and now here was a national district superintendent handling the services so very well, national Christians leading the singing and playing guitars, praying and organizing the services. She was overwhelmed! She exclaimed "Beautiful! I remember when even to the Christians, following Christ still seemed 'foreign,' but now I sense a depth of spirit and hunger for more of God's Spirit in many that I have talked with. I saw a growth of trees that made the scenery change, and I sensed a growth of spirit that made me know the church is changing too—in good ways. . . . I can do nothing except give praise for being allowed to be part of the beginning—and to share in this celebration of the 25th."

To close out the celebrations, a dinner was given in Wanda's honor at the Mount Hagen Hotel, and missionaries and their families and special friends of Wanda's from the European community gathered to give her tribute. After a sumptuous meal, her friends shared their special memories of Wanda in skits, songs, and poems. To remember Wanda was to remember the "open door policy" of her home; the ever-ready cup of coffee and—if you arrived at the right moment—one of her famous doughnuts. She had an ever-listening ear and would give a clasp on the shoulder, and a lift would come when you knew she'd interceded for you with her Heavenly Father. To remember Wanda was to remember her love for the Word and that special light in her eyes that came when she found a new nugget in that storehouse of treasure; the tennis games and walks in the moonlight; the Easter sunrise services and breakfast on the mountain; C. S. Lewis reviews; and her voice in lilting laughter, teasing words, or lovely song. Laughter and tears intermingled, and the evening concluded with a final tribute that confirmed the deep love all those present felt for Wanda: "Tonight we are celebrating an anniversary: 25 years of living and loving, of teaching and preaching, of building and training, and the end is not yet. We praise God for what has been accomplished. There had to be a beginning, and for that we give special tribute to Wanda tonight and deep heartfelt gratitude that God led you here and thus began the weaving that has intertwined all of our lives and produced what we see today. To God be the glory, and thank you, Wanda."

The delightful 10 days in Papua New Guinea ended all

too soon. Wanda noted in her diary, "It's almost impossible to put down how I really felt, but . . . it was a most beautiful time. I will live with that memory in my heart for many years. It was good to see the missionaries and other friends across the valley too. Another special gift from Him—and now on to Israel."

Wanda arrived in Tel Aviv on August 7 and was met by Merlin and Alice Hunter, missionaries serving in Nazareth, and Juanita Smith, who became a housemate and very dear friend. Juanita had been a volunteer in Israel since 1977 and then had been put on special assignment to help Wanda during the Morgans' furlough. Wanda experienced her first meal in Israel at Quicklys, a small Jewish restaurant that was to become a favorite place with its specialties of chicken livers, pita bread, and hummus, a salad of crushed chick-peas with olive oil and red paprika.

From pioneering in Papua New Guinea to pastoring in such a tourist spot as Jerusalem was not easy for Wanda. It was also difficult for a woman to have this kind of responsibility and authority in a very male-oriented society. In the beginning, some of the people had a real problem with this situation, but in a very short time Wanda had won their confidence and respect and was deeply loved by them. It wouldn't have worked out if God had not been directing all of the time.

Wanda loved the Sunday Schools out in the villages. Friday was the big Sunday School day in some of the villages, and as it was the Muslim day off, some of the Muslim children met with the other children for Bible stories. Wanda and Juanita always went a little early to allow time for buying fresh vegetables and fruit in the open-air markets. They would also buy fresh eggs and pick out the plumpest chicken, waiting for the vendors to kill it, drain, and pluck it.

Wanda also loved the Saturday afternoon services (mainly Arab and Armenian) in the Old City on Mount Zion. The people loved to sing, and one favorite chorus Wanda sang in pidgin and taught in English was, "Have I Not Told You That if You Believe, You'll See the Glory of God." Often as she labored, her heart would go out to the Morgans and the other missionaries who had labored so long and so hard for so little fruit. Such a ministry was not easy, but in spite of the difficulties, Wanda felt that God gave her a good year in many ways.

She met some wonderful people. She would cherish the friendships of Michael, a Russian Jew, and EmDeana, an Old City Armenian lady. Wanda and EmDeana couldn't carry on a conversation because of the language difference, but it was enough to communicate through a handshake and a smile and to know that each was praying for the other. There were Halla and Em Nabil and their families, Arabs in the Jerusalem church; and Araxie and Sarun, Armenians of Jericho. Araxie served as translator for the Saturday services in the Old City. There were encouraging prayer meetings and signs of God's Spirit working in the lives of the people.

She would also be able to complete 20 hours of college work at the Institute of Holy Land Studies while pastoring the church in Jerusalem. Going on field trips for the study of the history and geography of Israel gave her a new feel of the land. Traveling out the borders of the old tribal lines, she felt she was being transported centuries back. As Wanda traveled the dusty roads and walked beside the Sea of Galilee, she felt as if the Lord himself walked beside her, showing her His earthly homeplace.

She was almost intoxicated with the atmosphere of the Hebrew University library. She felt it was the best she had ever encountered. She would browse for hours for pleasure or do research intently on such projects as a paper on Islamic thought.

She enjoyed eating in the university cafeteria as well, but one day her presence almost created a riot. As she was getting her meal, she forgot and left her briefcase under the coffee urn. When someone saw it, unattended, they thought it was a bomb! People began getting up and leaving, not bothering to finish their meal. At last, an attendant came over to Wanda, who had not understood the Hebrew and asked her in English if the briefcase were hers. When she stood up to get it, everyone began to clap, and she, red-faced and embarrassed, retrieved the offending case.

Not long after Wanda arrived, she began making hot rolls for Sunday dinner. People who were invited back after already experiencing this delicious item, as they entered the living quarters from the stairwell of the church, would immediately look into the kitchen to see if they could spot the rolls. This became almost a weekly tradition accompanied with a dinner conversation about the writings of C. S. Lewis.

One morning about 3 A.M., Wanda was awakened by a very strange noise. She listened, and there was a tapping noise that sounded like it might be someone signaling to another person. Without turning any lights on, she took a flashlight in hand and went down three flights of stairs to Juanita's room. The roof was flat, and there was a utility room located there, so the ladies thought they should check out the situation. When they returned to Wanda's room, Juanita could also clearly hear the tapping. Armed with flashlight, broom handle, and a can of mace, they were ready to tackle whatever might be on the other side of the door. After they looked all around, much to their relief, they discovered the noise to be water dripping from a pipe onto a tin plate. The drip was slow but very steady, and it did sound like tapping. After it was all over, they enjoyed a good laugh, put the coffeepot on, and had a bowl of cereal. They certainly weren't sleepy after that experience!

Wanda had many unique experiences in Israel. Once she and Juanita were invited to go to Beersheba with a couple from the Christian and Missionary Alliance church to minister to some Bedouins. As they approached the tents, some women saw the car and put their veils over their faces because of a man being present. When the missionaries gave a friendly greeting of peace, they were immediately invited into the tent. Taking off their shoes, the group sat down on mats and enjoyed tea along with good fellowship and the sharing of the gospel. It was fascinating watching the women make a fire from a few pieces of wood and cardboard. One of the women then put some water into each of the glasses she was going to serve the tea in and, using her fingers, cleaned the inside and outside. When the water began to boil, she put loose tea and two handfuls of sugar into the pot and boiled the mixture a little longer. It was very sweet. They always serve from a tray, and if it is a friendly visit, they will serve three times. It would be impolite not to drink it.

One afternoon Wanda and Juanita were doing a little sight-seeing with Merlin and Alice Hunter in the city of Nain. There is a small Franciscan church built there in memory of the miracle performed by Jesus. They were walking through some high brush to take a picture of the church when Wanda stepped up on a rock wall and felt something, either a sting or a bite. At first she thought it was her toe, but then she found a mark halfway up her shin. Her foot and leg became numb, and she thought whatever it was must have put some poison into her system. She decided it might have been a scorpion. Juanita remembers, "Along the way to Mount Tabor a couple of miles away, we had prayed individually, but when we were in the Church of the Transfiguration, we collectively prayed, and Wanda began to feel a change right away. Within a few minutes the pain and discomfort had completely gone, and we thanked and praised God for His touch."

An added joy of the Israel experience was Janie's visit at Christmas. It was Wanda's delight to show Janie the sights and sounds of this lovely land. During Janie's two weeks there, they did much traveling. Shopping had always been a favorite pastime of Wanda's, and now she loved to wander through the many shops in the Old City, enjoying the bargaining even more than the shopping and usually able to get her bottom price. On shopping excursions, sometimes conversations would develop with the shopkeeper about everyday living and life in general. Living in Israel, one had to be careful how subjects of religion were handled. Wanda deftly handled such situations. A Muslim shopkeeper, who was a mystic, told what he experienced in his religion; and Wanda would say, "Ah, but you can have so much more." And then there was the Jewish craftsman who told her that his boy had just recently had his Bar Mitzvah and said, "Now his sins are upon his own head; I'm no longer responsible for him"; and Wanda replied, "And we have Someone that took our sins upon himself." As Wanda would share with Jews and Muslims, she would often turn and wipe the tears from her eyes because her heart was breaking as she listened to them share with her that they were doing and living the best they could. These believed in God but so much differently than she.

Janie, having become engaged to Dennis Norrick, also enjoyed making wedding plans with her mother. Wanda especially enjoyed the weddings she had attended while in Jerusalem, and she and Janie borrowed one of the Arab customs to use in Janie's wedding, planned for the following August. At Arabic weddings, guests took home candy in either plastic, glass, or brass dishes. Wanda wanted to incorporate a local tradition for Janie's wedding along with traditions of Papua New Guinea, so Wanda purchased small brass candy dishes for the adults and key rings carved out of olive wood in shapes of camels and stars for the children. Months later in Olathe, Kans., these gifts added a lovely dimension to Janie's wedding.

Following the year in Israel and after the wedding in August of 1981, Wanda moved to Bethany to continue her education in order to be able to offer herself to the World Mission Department as a supply missionary or in whatever capacity she was needed. She completed her A.B. degree during the fall semester and then worked on her master's degree during the spring and fall semesters of 1982. While at Bethany, she was in several classes with her nephew, Scott Meador. Scott affirmed that classes became more interesting and stimulating when Wanda was a part of them. She was very conservative theologically and willing to debate very intensely in religion classes, to the delight of the other students. Having taught so many years in the Australian system and being used to essay tests, she disliked objective tests, feeling that cramming for knowledge of dates and names did little to help one retain knowledge or achieve much learning. She never took a casual or apathetic view toward any course. She put forth as much effort in astronomy, exclaiming in delight at discoveries with her telescope, as she did poring over a text in apocalyptic literature.

Wanda became a part of Bethany First Church staff as college pastor while she was on campus. Though she established many close relationships with the college young people, she didn't always relate as she wished to because of her age and her removal from American culture for so many years. Wanda lived a very simple life-style and was often concerned at the affluence and materialism she saw among many of the students. She was also deeply concerned that spiritual experiences were shallow rather than a deep commitment to God. Her godly influence was felt on campus, and students like Gary Yarberry, now a pastor in Arkansas, said of her, "Wanda was an inspiring person who always exemplified the Servant, Jesus. I have wished many times to have the commitment level she possessed. Her dedication still speaks to me." Gary said he would always remember some counsel Wanda once gave him in a difficult decision that he was trying to make. She said, "When your head tells you one thing and your heart another, follow the voice of the heart." Gary said he had followed that advice in sermon preparation, preaching, visiting, board decisions, family matters, and many other areas of life and had never regretted following the "voice of the heart." Gary also commented, "I sometimes feel that she is watching over my shoulder to encourage me along. And I would be content to stay in her shadow throughout my ministry. Just as the shadow of Peter brought healing to others, the shadow of Mrs. Knox brought healing to a lot of people."

Wanda's achievements and influence upon the campus was remembered in 1984 when she was the recipient of the "B" award from Bethany Nazarene College for meritorious service.

Wanda's schooling was interrupted by another mission call, and this time she was appointed for a full term to the Caribbean Nazarene Theological College in the beautiful land of Trinidad. She left for Trinidad in February of 1983.

From Papua New Guinea to Israel to the Caribbean took a lot of adjusting. Different environments, different cultures, different languages evoked different responses. Both Wanda and the students at the seminary had lots to learn. Errol Carrim, one of her students, took Wanda's openness and friendliness as a front, and so when she asked to go with him to town to do some shopping, he thought she was kidding. Missionaries just didn't do that, so he left her. When he came back, she met him, arms akimbo, demanding, "Young man, you left me standing here. Why did you leave me?" Realizing her genuineness, Errol entered into a friendship that was to impact his life greatly.

Wanda added a refreshing dimension to the campus with her vitality, friendly hospitality, and her "tough love" that never felt tough because it was so loving. Her classes were stimulating and different. She read from Calvin Miller's *The Singer* every morning. It was the first time that Errol had ever experienced a perspective and interpretation of Christ other than the Bible, and it was very meaningful to him. Even today, he says whenever he sees that book, he thinks of Wanda. She introduced the students to C. S. Lewis and to Shakespeare. She encouraged the students to dramatize Shakespeare's works in class, and what a compliment it was to them when she told them they had done it well!

It was the little gestures of friendship that so endeared Wanda to Errol. He pastored a home mission church while in school and traveled to the church on public transport. Many a Sunday evening, coming in dead tired, he would go to his mailbox and there find a note of encouragement from Wanda. It was his dream that someday, when he finished his education, he and Wanda would teach in the seminary together. Expressing the influence of Wanda upon him, Errol said, "All of us in life have people we want to achieve for. In my background there was no one in particular, but I wanted to achieve for Wanda. I wanted to accomplish something for her."

Wanda's contacts with the students and with the people gave her great enjoyment and fulfillment, which helped to alleviate the distress and discouragement she sometimes felt in some of her circumstances. All of the water had to be boiled, and since she used most of hers in making drinks for others, she was always running out. There were extreme changes in the weather, and she was often awakened in the early morning by fierce storms. Travel was always difficult, and the roads were preposterous to her. Her classes really did drain her as she put in hours of work developing new curriculum. She missed the close relationships of previous years and said, "Sometimes I'd like to relax with someone I could talk to about anything, but I'm not complaining. I'm grateful to the Lord for the place He's given to me to serve."

While she was in Trinidad, she received exciting news from home. She shared in her diary, "Today Geron called. His voice was filled with excitement and pride. He and Loretta have been blessed with a healthy, beautiful (my eyes haven't seen her yet, but Geron says she's beautiful) baby girl—Lindsey Marie, 6 pounds 11 ounces—on November 6, 1983. My first grandchild! I have wanted a grandchild for quite a few years already, so how can I explain how I feel? I feel warm and happy and so tender, yet I ache inside too, to be so far away. The only comfort is in knowing I am where He wants me at the present time. But I am human enough to long to see and hold my precious granddaughter in my arms. Lindsey—I will be thinking of you so much and already (before you were born) I've been praying for you and will continue to do that, and your grandmother just wants you to know that you are so precious, so special, and I love you dearly. Even if I can't hold you in my arms—I hold you in my heart."

Wanda's heart was touched by the deep need around her. She picked up 12 children every Sunday morning for Sunday School. One of these youngsters crammed into her little car was Richard, a lad of about 14, who showed a great desire to go to church and to rise above his situation of deep poverty and evil influence.

Sickness and death ravaged the people. Once Wanda took a very ill student to a clinic. The nurse asked if the student were bleeding from the eyes, ears, or nose; and when Wanda said no, the nurse declared it was not an emergency and wouldn't see him. After a long wait, the guard at the clinic finally said, "He don't look sick to me!"

Wanda, incensed, said later, "I could have hit him!" Fortunately for all concerned, the student at last got the necessary medical treatment he required.

Wanda was also witness to the funeral of one of the pastor's sons. The pastor himself led the funeral, which was very different from those held in the States. The congregation participated by singing, even some peppy songs accompanied by hand clapping. An evangelistic sermon followed with an altar call. The grave had been dug, and the coffin was put to one side. After more songs and commitment of the body, everyone watched as the body was being lowered into the grave. One of the fellows assisting was drunk and singing while he lowered the body. The men put the dirt on the casket, and then everybody stepped up and dropped flowers on top. As this was being done, the father suddenly broke out in singing, "No more dying there, / We are going to see the King." With his face shining like an angel and joy in his voice, he seemed to embody the presence of God. It had an electrifying effect on those present. Wanda concluded: "They live a little closer to death than we do, and I think the way they handle death and conduct the services is better than we do."

While in Trinidad, Wanda was also able to go to Barbados for special services. Probably her most frustrating experience happened at that time. To get a visa for Barbados, she had to have a tax clearance with immigration. She hadn't been there to pay taxes the year before; and, though the mission was paying this year, there was confusion, and the officer in charge was not going to let her go. Packed and ready to go and committed to a missionary convention and several arranged services, she insisted she had to go. Since she was holding up the entire line, the officer sent her to the main immigration officer, who wasn't going to do anything either. In desperation Wanda burst into tears, which completely melted him. Later, on the plane, Wanda felt she had been deceitful and asked the Lord to forgive her. She told the Lord, "I didn't have to cry; I was frustrated, but not really teary, but I thought, I've got to show this guy how desperate I am!" Later in Barbados, she confessed to District Superintendent Greenidge, who laughed and laughed and teased Wanda when Mrs. Greenidge asked her to get up early to go shopping, "No tears now, no tears!"

Wanda loved the services in Barbados—the singing, clapping, and playing of tambourines, the dancing down the aisles. Wanda exclaimed, "I love, just love it! They praise the Lord so uninhibitedly. They do more congregational singing, fewer specials. I like that." At the missionary convention a dramatic flair was added by having people dressed up to represent Mr. General Budget, Miss NWMS, Mr. Prayer and Fasting, etc. They rode in cars to the church, escorted by a policeman who was saluting everyone and beating back the crowd who were trying to see the VIPs. It reminded Wanda of the times she as a young person would so enjoy the District Assembly. These people seemed so relaxed, seemed to be having so much fun, and seemed to be so enjoying the Lord.

In December of 1983, Wanda had her Christmas break all planned. She had been invited to six different homes for a "day" during the holidays. Also she had paint on hand and was planning to paint her kitchen and bathroom during her days off. She was looking forward to relaxing and doing a lot of swimming, but her well-laid plans were interrupted. She began feeling very tired but thought it was the humidity. Then she noticed a large bulge in her abdomen. She thought it was the middle-aged spread and that she was just getting fat but decided to check with a doctor. The doctor, discovering a large mass, wanted to operate right away, but Wanda decided to return to the States to have the surgery. Kathy Butts, hearing the news in Kansas City, was stunned and called Trinidad immediately to talk to Wanda. Wanda seemed quite calm and in complete control of the situation. She mentioned that she would need a doctor in Kansas City, since Dr. Howard Hamlin had been her doctor before she left. Now with his death, she would need another. Wanda had made her plans. She told Kathy, "I'll fly to Oklahoma City on Christmas Day to be with my folks for the holidays. Then I will come on to Kansas City to see the doctor there. Will you care for me if I have to have surgery?"

On Christmas Day, Wanda experienced her first Christmas dinner in the air. She enjoyed the few days with her mom and dad and had the unexpected pleasure of seeing Janie and Dennis who were at her mom's. Then the holidays were over, and she made her way to Kansas City. Kathy met her at the airport, and they went to a special restaurant on the way home. Wanda's appetite was as good as ever, and she loved to eat. She had chosen her doctor, who was the one that had cared for Dr. Hamlin during his illness. That first night after her arrival in Kansas City, she and Kathy talked most of the night. It was a beautiful talk about death and dying and heaven and grace and all the wonderful things Christians have to look forward to, even in the face of adversity or sickness. They shared deeply their common beliefs in prayer for healing and intercession. It was a precious time of heart fellowship.

The visit to the doctor was a bit tense for both Kathy and Wanda. Wanda was a little nervous, mostly because of the new doctor. She came from the examining room and admitted that surgery was inevitable. But she was quite pleased with her doctor. Even though he was a Hindu, they immediately shared in deep discussion about religious matters and their own personal beliefs. Kathy observed, "She never did wait long to get on those subjects!"

In January 1984 Wanda wrote, "Only He knows what '84 holds for me. But you know, He's been in control of my life for a long time now, and I feel confident that He is in control now regardless of the outcome. I only pray that He will give me strength to glorify Him in all things. Really, to live or die matters not if we really believe what we say we believe! And in my heart there's a deep, deep peace—in spite of the human reluctance to face suffering. I love Him more each day."

Surgery was scheduled for Tuesday, January 10. Wanda's testimony and faith were anchored upon God's Word, and she entered the operating room with His promise: "'For I know the plans I have for you,' declares the Lord, 'plans to prosper you and not to harm you, plans to give you hope and a future'" (Jer. 29:11, NIV).

9

A Name Written Down in Glory

THE SHRILL JANGLING of the telephone broke the silence of the hospital room. It was the first sound to reach Wanda's consciousness as she came out from under the anesthetic following her surgery. Then she heard Geron's voice in conversation with the caller. "Not too good—it was malignant, and they didn't get it all." Later, reliving those moments, Wanda shared in her diary, "It would be impossible to explain the depth of peace that flooded me at that moment. I have looked back to it many times since. I didn't know what all the future might hold, but at that point, all that mattered was that He was holding me—and He still is."

The waiting room was jammed with family and friends also awaiting the surgery results. When they received the news, they cried. There were tears of relief that the surgery was over but sorrow that the malignant tumors were not completely removed. There were tears of hope at the news that with chemotherapy there was a chance of recovery. There were tears of pain as those who loved her realized she had more suffering ahead of her.

When everyone but Kathy was gone, late in that first night after surgery, Wanda said into the darkness, "How bad was it? Tell me everything." And Kathy did, for they had agreed before surgery that nothing would be withheld from Wanda. Kathy explained the extent of the invasion of the ovarian carcinoma but also the good news that the implants that could not be removed had not penetrated into any other vital areas. Several times during the night, Wanda woke up and asked more questions, but the peace that flooded her soul in those first moments of recuperation held her in the days that followed.

Wanda's recovery from the surgery was quite normal. She wrote letters, received visitors, and generally kept everyone cheered up. In a letter written in February 1984, she assured her friends, "I'm in good health—other than this 'invader'—so the doctor is conservatively optimistic. I will be taking chemotherapy (once every three weeks) for six months. After three months and then again after six months another series of tests will be run, and if by then, nothing is found to be growing, they may do a second surgery to just see what is happening inside—to see if the implants are drying up. . . . I won't deny the change of direction has been difficult, perhaps because it was so sudden. I've delighted in teaching in Trinidad. I've loved the students and the people, and I miss them immensely. But then, what a joy to be able to pray for them personally along with others that I've been with in Israel and in Papua New Guinea. I feel at peace about it. I'm still where I have been for many years now—in His hands."

Life had become different for Wanda from what it had ever been before. It was the first time she could remember not having time limits. She tired easily and so did a lot of resting, hoping it would speed her recovery. She delighted in the close association with Geron and his family during these weeks of recovery.

Wanda loved to play with her granddaughter, Lindsey, and to work on her "Grandma's Book." Lindsey loved her special times with "Maamaw" Wanda. Wanda, sitting in her big chair, would place a blanket at her feet where Lindsey would play contentedly. One evening Geron and Loretta brought pizza (Lindsey's favorite food) to Wanda's house. Wanda could eat only soup. Lindsey, settled at "Maamaw's" feet, ready to eat pizza, suddenly realized that "Maamaw" had soup—not pizza! "Want soup, want soup!" Lindsey protested. Wanda, immensely thrilled, had Kathy discard the pizza, and grandmother and granddaughter shared the invalid fare that had turned into a special treat.

It was also during this time of recovery that Wanda received the joyous news of Janie's pregnancy, and Wanda was exultant. "My blessings are coming quickly. I am so happy for you and am looking forward to holding this second grandchild in my arms." Inspired by these events, Wanda took advantage of extra time to write special letters to her grandchildren to be opened when they reached the age of 10.

When Wanda was recovered to the point that chemotherapy could begin, her life-style changed drastically. Her will to cooperate with everything medical science offered was amazing. These were difficult days. Early on Monday mornings, she would enter the hospital for several hours of chemotherapy. She would be violently ill on the way home from the hospital and for several hours following until sleep finally came. About 2:00 in the morning, she would awaken and ask for a couple of sips of juice and two tablespoons of cooked cereal. She was motivated to get back on her feet as soon as possible. For three or four days following each treatment, her strength would be almost gone, but she pushed and forced herself to eat in order to keep in the best health possible. Between treatments, she and Kathy would travel around Missouri and Kansas, building up her physical strength. It helped her to cope, and Kathy remembers how much fun they had even in the midst of a most trying time.

Along with the sickness from the chemotherapy came the usual reaction of hair loss. Kathy remembers standing behind Wanda as she tried on wigs. Tears poured down Wanda's face, and that day a complete stranger sat down beside her, took off her own wig, and shared her experience. Wanda immediately responded with a positiveness about the hair loss—a positiveness that carried her through to the time she removed her wig for the last time.

Wanda's second surgery was scheduled in October. About two weeks before the surgery, a letter came to Wanda from Kaye Williams. She and her husband were finishing their second term as missionaries in Taiwan. Wanda was surprised to find that she was a very special person to Kaye. Kaye shared that she had felt God's gentle urging to write to Wanda to let her know she was praying for her, to encourage her, and to tell her that actually Wanda had had a lot to do with Kaye's being in Taiwan.

The story unfolded that Kaye as a child had read Wanda's book, *Pioneers to New Guinea,* written for the junior missionary series. It had tugged at her heart and confirmed a mission call in her life. She had told her family and classmates at school, that when she grew up, she was going to be a missionary. She got Wanda's address at that time to write and let her know too. Kaye's mother was happy for her to write, but she tried to allay the possible disappointment of not receiving an answer by reminding Kaye of missionaries' busy schedules. However, a few weeks later, a letter from New Guinea came, and as Kaye said, "You just can't imagine how excited I was." God reminded Kaye of her call many times while she was growing up, but by the time she got into college, she had almost convinced herself that she could do God's work just as well at home. The night came, though, that God made it crystal clear to her that she should be a missionary. He took her on a journey through her memory back to the little girl reading the missionary book that was indeed a guidepost of His leading in her life. Kaye shared, "From that point until now, it's been wonderful just feeling the sweet, assuring leadership of God in my life. I just wanted to write and thank you for your part in the whole thing. Sometimes the enemy tries to get us down and make us think that it has all been in vain. But often there are people being touched by our lives when we are not aware of it at all. Thank you for touching my life—in an indirect, but very real way. I pray for you during your illness. I am claiming Jer. 29:11 for you, '"For I know the plans I have for you," declares the Lord, "plans to prosper you and not to harm you, plans to give you hope and a future"'" (NIV).

Wanda laid the letter down, tears flowing freely as she thanked God for confirming His word to her again at that very time through someone so very far away. She had begun the year with that very promise. She had never claimed the promise as complete healing but felt it was God's special way of telling her that she was His, that she was still in His hands and His plans, and that, whatever the future held, it would come out to good—whether here on earth or on the other side. Knowing God was in control was all that mattered. As Wanda stated in a letter following her surgery, "After all, isn't our purpose to fulfill His will in our lives and to glorify Him? He can help us do that whatever circumstances allow."

Having such faith enabled Wanda to say, "So when the doctor spoke in my ear as I was coming around . . . saying everything was all right . . . and then later as all the pathology reports came back completely negative, and they found no trace of the cancer left . . . I found that the joy of thinking of a healthy body again was rather overshadowed by that still 'deep peace' that He had already given for months. I found myself praying, 'Well, Lord, Your plans must include some things You still have for me to do here. Keep me sensitive to You, and don't let me disappoint You!'"

The official report on the second surgery was a complete remission, but it would not be called a cure until at least five years had passed. During the first year, she was to have tests and scans about every three months and then have to be tested only once a year.

Wanda's rejoicing was cut short by the news of her father's illness. Just the day after she had her stitches out, she flew to Oklahoma City to be with her dad. They had a beautiful two hours of fellowship together, and then he was gone. Wanda expressed that she would always be grateful that the Lord let her get there in time.

By November, Wanda was resuming her normal lifestyle and busy schedule. Helen Bolerjack had returned to the States for the birth of her grandchild, Sarah Mealiff, and remembers Wanda insisting they have lunch, though Wanda had sat up all night at the bedside of a dear friend who had undergone surgery. Helen reminisced, "I'm glad she did. During our very lengthy conversation, she shared with me, among other things, how the Lord had given her such a deep, deep peace that was so precious and real that it was difficult to describe." Wanda was also able to travel to Texas and welcome her new grandson, Aaron Norrick, into the world. She enjoyed a wonderful Christmas with her family and busily made plans to attend seminary in the early part of 1985 while regaining her strength, her health, and her hair!

During the 10 months following her second surgery, Wanda was completely free from chemotherapy, and what a joy that was to her! Her strength returned rapidly, and she enjoyed a semester of study at seminary and made several trips to speak in various Faith Promise conventions. The 1985 General Assembly in Anaheim was a great blessing to her. She met and visited with many friends from across the years and arranged both Trinidad and Papua New Guinea reunions. With no responsibilities but to visit, worship, and praise the Lord, she experienced great joy. Following General Assembly, she spent several days in

Texas "drinking in" her precious grandson, Aaron. Remembering that visit, she wrote in her diary, "Aaron, 'bearer of light'—I pray he will always be just that. . . . What fun it is to be with you and hold you. You are growing so and have one of the most delightful personalities. I hope you will always stay sweet and loving."

After she returned home, a routine CAT scan revealed a small shadow. Surgery was scheduled for early August. Only Geron and Janie, Kathy and Dr. Nees, executive director of World Mission, knew of this new development. It was thought to be a small, benign tumor. Wanda noted in her diary, "They have found something in the scans. It doesn't seem to be going away, so the tumor board has decided surgery is the best option. If it's benign, they'll take it out, and my plans to go to Bethany and on to Trinidad will remain unchanged. If it's malignant . . . well, decisions will have to then be made. How do I feel? A little drained. It's not necessarily easy living with this constant possibility. However, the deep, inner feeling of peace remains."

Twenty minutes after surgery began, the surgeon called Kathy to come to the Consultation Room. He advised that the cancer had returned, and a colostomy was absolutely necessary. He was devastated himself, since both the surgeon and the oncologist were especially fond of this vibrant missionary, who challenged their medical knowledge, along with their thoughts about God, His universe, and His creation.

The first night of this last surgery, when all company had gone for the night, Wanda rallied and said, "How bad is it?" She and Kathy called the cancer "gremlins," and Kathy shared with her that the gremlins had returned. She slept awhile longer, then asked, "What else?" When Kathy told her she had a colostomy, she inquired as to whether it was temporary or permanent, still holding on to recovery. Kathy remembers, "When I told her it was irreversible, a dark cloud came over that room, and I knew a battle raged within. It took her two days to come to grips with her situation. But she soon had it handled with that undefeatable spirit to make the most of what was left!"

Wanda's Hindu doctor called her, the children, and Kathy into consultation and shared that all had been done that could be done. Weeping unashamedly, he said he would do all that he could to make her comfortable and confessed, "As you know, we are very fond of this woman."

In September, Wanda sent a form letter to her friends, informing them of her condition at the time. She went on treatment from M. D. Anderson Cancer Institute of Houston. It was an experimental drug, and no one was sure of the outcome, but she assured her friends that, though her circumstances had changed again, God had not, and her promise from Jeremiah was more precious than ever, a constant that would continue through eternity. In this letter, she also shared a song that had been used in a girls' trio during college days. She had been a member of the trio, and Sidney had accompanied them. The practice of the day was to sing only three verses of a song, but each girl, as well as Sidney, had claimed a verse of this particular song, and none of them were willing to leave their verse out, so they always sang all four verses. Wanda reminisced, "I recently came across this song again, and as I read the verses, my heart rejoiced anew in the message of it, and somehow I just felt I wanted to share it with you at this time, for I still believe He is working out His purpose."

God Is Working Out His Purpose

God is working out His purpose
  He has planned for you and me;
Though from us it may be hidden,
  Someday we shall plainly see
How He stands behind the shadows,
  Waiting to perform His will,
Whisp'ring, "Child, be of good courage;
  Ev'ry promise I'll fulfill."

God is working out His purpose,
  Even though we go alone;
It may take us from our loved ones,
  Lead us far away from home.
It will be the greatest pleasure,
  Just to feel His presence near,
And to know that God is working
  Out the purpose to Him dear.

God is working out His purpose
  Though it lead through desert bare;
He'll go with us on life's journey,
  And our heavy burdens share.
Through the weary years of waiting,
  When the heart cries, "Lord, how long?"
God is working out His purpose;
  Right will triumph over wrong.

God is working out His purpose.
  Never murmur nor repine,
For our future's in His keeping;
  Gladly to His will resign.

When the veil at last is lifted,
And the shadows flee away,
We shall understand His purpose
Through one glad, eternal day.

—Mrs. F. W. Suffield

The months that followed are permanently engraved in the memory of those who surrounded Wanda during those days. They will remember a woman who believed God to the end. No amount of pain could make her doubt His love. Though there were times she rocked on her knees in agony, she knew He was still holding her in His hands. The doctors agreed that the experimental treatment from Houston was not being effective, as fluid built up, and Wanda had to have fluid removed from her abdomen about twice a week. Many emergency runs were made in the middle of the night when it seemed she was at the point of death. Kathy vividly remembers one such time, when after another crisis had been averted, Wanda, feeling much better, said she was hungry. She sent Kathy out for Mexican food and, when Kathy brought it, "wolfed" it down with the hospital room suddenly filled with the wonderful odor of Mexican food.

Thanksgiving time drew near, and, though Wanda was very weak, the whole family was coming in to celebrate. Wanda was so looking forward to it and hoping it would be one of her good days. Donna Fillmore's Sunday School class of sixth grade girls took Wanda's Thanksgiving celebration on as a special prayer project. In their classroom each week they placed a rose to represent Wanda, and they would pray that she would have appetite enough to enjoy her Thanksgiving meal and strength to enjoy the fellowship of her loved ones. Their prayers were answered. Wanda enjoyed her dinner immensely and was able to sit up and talk and laugh and play games with her children and grandchildren. Later, she sent a card of thanks to the girls: "I want to thank you so much for your precious prayers for me. I especially wanted you to know that this week has been perfect. I have felt so good and enjoyed my family so much on Thanksgiving Day. I'm sure God answered your prayers."

Also in November, Wanda dropped a note to Nina Gunter, executive director of NWMS, apologizing for an uncompleted writing assignment. Wanda explained that she didn't have the strength or concentration to write the article; but she did want to share some words about how the medical plan had helped her, and perhaps her thanks could be shared in an article. Up to that point, Wanda figured her medical costs had been close to $50,000. Wanda exclaimed, "What would I have done if our people had not provided for their missionaries an adequate medical plan? I think that I've only had to pay around $300 a year out of my own pocket for medical expenses since I've been ill! To fight the illness has not been easy—to have had to worry about finances would have been terrible. Oh, how grateful I am to our people around the church who love us and believe in the call of missions and are willing to support us in salaries, in prayer, in extras like LINKS and Medical Plan. I could never thank them enough."

The Deasleys ministered to Wanda during her illness in a special way. Wanda had brought Alex a Communion set from Jerusalem, and she enjoyed taking Communion in one of those cups. One day during a time of extreme weakness when she was barely able to lift her hand, during the

Communion service while Alex prayed, she sat bolt upright. Remembering the electrifying presence of the Holy Spirit, Joyce said, "I thought she was going to get up!" Heaven came near.

Wanda directed Christmas activities from her big chair, and though Donna Fillmore addressed her cards, Wanda wrote the notes. In a parting thoughtful gesture to the Deasleys, she sent a basket of delicacies—things that would please a Scotsman's palate, such as Vegemite, Marmite, and special jams. Knowing the end was near, Wanda began to designate pictures on the wall or dishes she wanted to give to her friends.

Wanda was very realistic about death. She acknowledged its ugliness but was very positive about the final outcome. She penned this original verse in her diary:

I used to think—loving life so greatly—
That to die would be like leaving a party
Before the end.
Now I know that the "party"
Is really happening somewhere else;
That the light and the music—
Escaping in snatches
To make the pulse beat
And the tempo quicken—
Come from a long way away.
And I know too
That when I get there,
The music (and praise to Him)
Will never end.

In the last days Wanda's feet would swell, and Kathy had to continually buy her larger slippers. One day, Wanda looked at her feet that were turning black and said, "I'm dying, Kathy." Those who saw her in that last week realized death was near, but Wanda's indomitable spirit shone through. Miriam Hall remembers going by the Sunday night before Wanda's death to say good-bye, and after they talked, Wanda said, "But, we'll meet again," and laughed out loud.

Linda Mealiff went by to see Wanda and was shocked to find her totally unrecognizable. She had literally wasted away, but when she smiled, the recognition came and she was "Aunt Wanda." Though Wanda was drowsy because of the medication, she was coherent, and they talked for a while. Even at this critical stage, Wanda was grateful for many things. She was so thankful she could stay home. She had nursing care around the clock and was concerned for her nurses. Kathy was a pillar of strength and stability to her at this time. Wanda accepted her oncoming death better than anyone else. She planned her funeral and remained her cheerful, trusting self, believing God would take care of her. She would say, "I just want to die like a Christian." Rather than being concerned for herself, she was concerned for the spiritual welfare of her children and grandchildren and how they would adjust without her. Linda knew she'd never see Wanda alive again. Realizing she was the representative on location of all the MKs this lovely lady had loved and encouraged through the years, she struggled to say thanks. Inarticulate with grief, all she could say was, "I love you."

Early on Friday morning, January 3, 1986, Kathy and Geron were at Wanda's side, where they had been all night. Wanda had taken minimal morphine for her pain, for she wanted to be alert to the end. Kathy and Geron were holding her hands when she roused and said, "Let go of my hands," and then lay back, and it was over. Wanda had escaped the bonds of illness, pain, and suffering and walked into His presence.

Two hours later Errol Carrim, one of Wanda's former students in Trinidad, called, and when he heard the news, sobbed openly over the phone. Errol says that Wanda's death was one of the greatest losses in his life. In 1984, even while she was ill, she had worked with Errol through the Sidney Knox Foundation and through scholarships to bring him to the States to further his education. She had made it possible for him to come to Eastern Nazarene College, and through these last two years they'd talked on the phone and exchanged cards and letters but had not met face-to-face since they had been in Trinidad. He didn't have money to come to the funeral, but as he expressed it, "Memories are what you remember, not someone in a casket. I had the plaque she'd given me that said, 'The will of God will never lead you where His grace can't keep you,' and a water jug to remember her by." It seemed so strange that she'd died.

Helen Temple, in her tribute to Wanda in the *Standard,* spoke of the legacy Wanda left for us all—"the triumph of faith in God over the worst that Satan can fling at us." This was the theme of her funeral service at Olathe College Church on January 6, 1986. It was a joyful celebration, planned by Wanda and carried out by those who loved her. Trust, faith, and joy were proclaimed from the musical prelude to the final benediction. After reading the promise from Jer. 29:11 that Wanda had held onto during her months of illness, Pastor Paul Cunningham declared, "Today she lives out that future with her blessed Lord whom she will be with forever, and one day we will all be together again."

Dr. Charles Strickland, representing the Board of General Superintendents, spoke of the legacy left by Wanda. "Her missionary passion and gracious spiritual warmth won the admiration of the entire church in North America. Her dedication and her commitment awakened in our youth a desire to serve God, and there are many young missionaries today who testify to receiving their call in a convention led by Wanda. Wanda Knox has given to the Church of the Nazarene a modern example of what a totally dedicated life can give to advance the kingdom of God. . . . A great host of people will rise to call blessed this beautiful handmaiden of the Lord who brought light to so many who were in spiritual darkness, particularly those from the mountain jungle of Papua New Guinea whom the world had forgotten. . . . It is our trust and hope that the church will never allow to be forgotten this beautiful life so dedicated to Christ and the church that she so greatly loved."

Dr. Phyllis Perkins, who followed Wanda in the position of executive director of NWMS, wrote a tribute to Wanda that was read at the funeral and that spoke of Wanda pouring her life into NWMS. Dr. Perkins said Wanda would be remembered most for her missionary spirit, her passion for lost souls that she transmitted to missionary societies throughout the international church. Dr. Perkins remembered that when Wanda was orienting her to the director's office, she had said, "When I came to Kansas City in 1975, my missionary vision was primarily for Papua New Guinea; then after a short time, I began to feel the burden for the whole world." Dr. Perkins said, "In her gen-

124

uine enthusiastic way, she helped all of us catch more of that vision that permeated her life. I have trouble keeping this letter in the past tense. Wanda is very much alive for me, and I celebrate her homegoing and her freedom from pain. Today, Wanda is still with us in her investment and legacy of the missionary vision. We cannot forget her unselfish total commitment to God's call to serve, nor can we fail to respond to His clear commission for us."

Dr. Cunningham's prayer declared, "If God can so mightily equip her, so mightily empower her, there is hope for us that Your Holy Spirit can do in and through us what You did in and through her. So help us, O Lord, today not to waste the lessons that You want us to learn through her life and through her death."

And that determination was felt even as the service continued. Linda Mealiff said, "The most significant part of the funeral to me was the song 'Until Then.'" Linda said then her heart was flooded with joy. Everything was now all right. Finally, Wanda was home, and Linda would go on singing; she would carry on. That legacy of faith prepared her in a few months to empathize with her husband in the loss of his father. It helped her enable her children to deal with grief.

It enabled Errol Carrim six months later to really deal with and accept her death. At that time he was enrolled in Nazarene Theological Seminary. Coming to Kansas City held much meaning for him. It was not just to obtain an education. It was coming to where Wanda had been. It was seeing the places she had seen, sitting in classrooms and thinking Wanda had been there, worshiping in church and thinking, Wanda praised the Lord here. He became involved in a chaplaincy program as part of his practics class, and it was ironic that he was assigned as a chaplain in a cottage where three boys had lost their mothers. These were the only ones in this situation, and he had had to deal personally with Wanda's death as he counseled these boys in their loss. At last he had to recognize his own loss and put it into the hands of God.

That legacy was reflected in Dr. Orville Jenkins's funeral message as he told of his encounter with Merilyn Wutsik, daughter of one of the first converts of Sidney and Wanda's ministry. Merilyn had said, "My mother heard the message of salvation through the lips of Sidney and Wanda Knox. I was taken to Sunday School and church as a very young child. I too met Jesus, and my life has been totally changed by the gospel." When Dr. Jenkins had asked Merilyn to give one word of what the coming of the missionaries had meant, she answered, "Hope. I was given hope where there was no hope."

That legacy would raise up a Wanda Knox Memorial Fund that now has reached over $75,000 to further mission education around the world. A memorial chapel would be built on the campus of Nazarene Bible College in Papua New Guinea. This simply designed but beautiful and worshipful building is a fitting tribute to Wanda, who experienced one of her greatest delights in teaching and training young pastors. Already many hearts have been blessed and lives changed as they have gathered in this chapel and sensed the power and presence of the Holy Spirit in their lives.

The benediction prayed at Wanda's funeral continues to be answered: "The powerful change that You made in Wanda's life, which enabled her to pour out her life as a drink offering to God, has been used by the Holy Spirit to

Wanda Knox Memorial Chapel

change countless lives. She lived with great purpose, and may we in these days of our lives find great purpose in living; may we share the mission You gave her to reach the whole world with the gospel."

And, looking down from her heavenly pew, Wanda said, "Amen."